ANNE SAFRANYOS
CHARTERED FINANCIAL PLANNER
BRANCH MANAGER

REGAL CAPITAL PLANNERS LTD.
2407 DOUGALL AVENUE
WINDSOR, ONTARIO   N8X 1T3
BUS. 972-1520   RES. 966-7849
FAX 972-1523

The
Wealthy
Barber

*The Common Sense Guide
to Successful Financial Planning*

by David Chilton

Financial Awareness Corporation

Editor:	Susan Daminato
Cover Design:	Chuck Temple
Book Design:	jg publishing services inc.
Printing:	Johanns Graphics Inc.

Canadian Cataloguing in Publication Data

Chilton, David Barr
  The wealthy barber

ISBN 0-9693557-1-8 (bound)   ISBN 0-9693557-0-X (pbk.)

1. Finance, Personal. I. Title.

HG179.C45 1988   332.024′01   C88-094913-9

To Susan

PREFACE

The wisest tips on how to develop a financial plan are of little use if they are not conveyed in an understandable manner – a manner that responds effectively to the questions and concerns of the reader. Likewise, the most articulately expressed thoughts on finance may be wasted if they are not presented in an entertaining style – a style that maintains the interest of the reader.

So, how does one write an understandable and entertaining financial planning book?

I hope, and believe, that *The Wealthy Barber* answers that question.

I wish you good reading, and good planning!

David Chilton

CONTENTS

1
THE FINANCIAL ILLITERATE

I love April. I wouldn't trade it for two of any other month. Except, perhaps, for October. Two Octobers would mean twice as many birthday presents – and Oktoberfests!

Why April? Weather-wise, it offers neither the best of summer nor the best of winter. It certainly doesn't provide the beauty of the fall months. Is it because, at least to poets and romantics, it symbolizes a new beginning, a kind of rebirth?

No.

I love April for three reasons: the National Basketball Association playoffs, the National Hockey League playoffs, and the essence of life itself – a new Major League Baseball season. Ah, April. Paradise on earth!

Thanks to my convertor, I can sit motionless, flicking back and forth between the NBA on TSN and the NHL on CBC, while listening to my beloved Tigers winning on one radio and the despised Blue Jays losing on another. When you throw in a second TV and a VCR, the possibilities are endless.

In addition to being professional sports' finest hour, April also ushers in the start of the golf season and marks the return of Ontario's fastest-growing religion – slo-pitch.

Needless to say, my wife, Susan, is not quite as fond of April as I am. However, even she would rank it among her favourite months. She is a fine tennis player, and April brings with it the first opportunity in half a year to hit the ball around. She also loves lawn work and spends a great deal of time in our garden. I use the word "our" loosely.

Surprisingly, slo-pitch season is something Susan enjoys as much as I do, if not more. The thirteen guys on our team range in age from twenty-eight to thirty-two, with me being the youngest. Seven are married and three have children. Tournaments, barbecues, pool parties, and evenings at our sponsor's – a terrific bar in Waterloo – are the highlights of the summer. All the wives and girlfriends get along famously. In fact, they appear to hold contests to see who can sit in the stands and pay the least attention to the game. Inevitably, when a game ends, the first thing our devoted fans ask is, "Who won?"

This April, though, is a little different from Aprils gone by. Sue is pregnant, or as she likes to put it, "we" are pregnant. If it's true that we are pregnant, it is also true that I am handling it better than Sue. I am seldom tired and I haven't gained a single pound over the first five months.

Actually, Sue is handling the pregnancy very well. She is a beautiful woman who prides herself on her appearance, so she has kept herself in excellent shape. As for being tired, no way. She's too excited. I'm sure every woman feels that way when she's about to have a baby, especially her first, but Sue is in a different league. One week after our doctor's confirmation, she had completely furnished and decorated a nursery. We have also bought a complete set of encyclopedia. You never know when a child may feel a need to refer to an authority greater than his parent.

Our decision to have children was easy. Both Sue and I love kids. In a way, that's ironic because we both come from small families. Sue is an only child, and I have just one sibling. At thirty, my sister Cathy is two years older than I am but, because of our months of birth, she registered in school only one year before me. Much to everyone's surprise, I accelerated through grades three and four and caught up to her. This is something I have never let her forget.

As I said, deciding to have children was easy. Barring unforeseen events, we plan on having three. Mind you, if they're all girls, we will keep on going indefinitely. When friends ask me what sex I hope this one is, I always reply, "I don't care...as long as it's a healthy boy."

Maybe I long for a son because I think that I could relate better to a boy and thus be a better parent. Maybe it's the old *carry-on-the-family-name* / *I-want-to-be-immortal* mentality. Then again, maybe Sue's right. It could just be so that I can play in the annual father-and-son golf tournament, and miss another weekend of yard work each year. So much for Freud.

Without a doubt, the highlight of the pregnancy to this point has been the reaction of the four first-time grandparents-to-be. Each excited couple phones at least once every forty-eight hours to see how Susan feels and to make sure I'm doing the housework and treating her well. This wouldn't bother me if it were only her parents questioning my abilities as a husband, but my parents are even worse. Dad says that Mom fainted when Susan told her I shampooed the rugs, and I'm not at all sure he's kidding.

Truthfully, helping with housework has been a great learning experience – not a great experience, but a great learning experience. I now know the origin of the expression, "A woman's work is never done." My wife, for example, works as a travel agent from nine 'til five, comes home, cooks a meal, does laundry, and works out. I can understand why she always hits the sack at ten-thirty. I've been out like a light by nine since I reluctantly volunteered to do some of the household tasks.

I can't defend my previous lack of respect for housework. And I don't have to. It's my mother's fault. The wife of a high school principal, she has never held a paying job. As with most of their contemporaries, Dad brought home the bacon and Mom cooked it. While he was at work, Mom would do all the household chores, leaving her evenings free.

To my great pleasure, I was asked to do very little. While other kids mowed the lawn or shoveled snow, I chased down fly balls or played road-hockey. I'm not sure why my parents were so easy on me but, to this day, I appreciate it.

On the other hand, Sue's parents, bucking the *spoil-the-only-child* stereotype, raised Sue to be a diligent worker. And to this day, I appreciate **that** even more! By the time we were married, she was used to doing housework and preparing meals. Being used to something, though, and enjoying it are far from synonymous. Now that I have come to realize just how much drudgery is involved in running a home, I am determined to become a *new and improved* person.

The guys on the slo-pitch team have started a pool, betting on how long the *new me* will last. Our pitcher informs me that the longest guess is four months; that is, until Sue is no longer pregnant. The shortest prediction, three weeks, was submitted by my wife. Now that's confidence.

As if taking it from the guys on the team two nights a week isn't bad enough, this weekend I'm going to get it from the future grandparents – live. As is our custom on the third weekend of each month, Sue and I are heading to Sarnia.

However, there's no need to feel sorry for us. Really. We go willingly. Both of us were born and raised there. Yes, it is an industrial town, and yes, it does have a distinct aroma. But Sarnia is not the grimy, run-down town non-Sarnians might imagine it to be – not at all. During my youth, its annual per capita income was consistently among the highest in Ontario. And believe me, the smoke and smell of the refineries are more than offset by the beauty of Lake Huron and the friendliness of the people.

If I seem defensive about Sarnia, it's because I am. In terms of diversification and growth potential, it certainly is no match for our current home, Kitchener. But there is something special about a hometown, especially one on the water. Sarnia comes alive in the summer. It's one continuous party, and to kids and teenagers that's pretty appealing.

In fact, that's pretty appealing to adults too, us included. That's why, this summer, Sue and I are spending five weeks at a rented cottage just outside Sarnia, in Bright's Grove.

I've been teaching for four years now, and every summer I have either taken a course or taught one. But this year, with the baby due in early September, we elected to keep the summer open and head for the cool water.

Sue is ecstatic. There's a seasonal slowdown in the travel business so, like me, she has July and August off every year. Her friends, however, do not. So, those summers that I've been studying, working and golfing, she has often been forced to spend time alone, burning, peeling and reading. I'm making it sound worse than it has been. As an independent woman, she has pursued several hobbies and interests. Nevertheless, she is really looking forward to seeing her two best friends and mother every day for five weeks this summer.

Initially, Sue's enthusiasm far outweighed mine. I have a great many friends in Sarnia, but only one of them is a teacher. Sure, Scott might be good for eighteen every morning – but who would I tee off with in the afternoons?

The more I thought about it, though, the more I warmed up to the idea. My best friend, Tom Garrett, is taking a holiday from his job at the refinery for the last three weeks of our stay. Tom loves to golf, go to Detroit Tiger games, lie on the beach, and quaff a few cold ones. In my book, the guy is perfect.

When Sue and I go to Sarnia for the weekend, we follow a fairly set routine.

We arrive Friday night at around eight-thirty. We usually go straight to my parents' house and enjoy a leisurely dinner. Then at ten-thirty, we go out to join some of our friends.

Saturday, Sue disappears. She does not save this act exclusively for Sarnia. In the four years we've been married, I've seen her only a dozen times on a Saturday afternoon – always at weddings. I'm not exactly sure where she goes, but it must be somewhere magical because invariably, when she returns, her shoes appear to have changed colours.

While she is AWOL – Absent With Our Loot – I spend the day with Tom. We meet my sister Cathy for breakfast at the Chalet Restaurant at nine o'clock sharp. Depending on what we did Friday night after leaving my parents, this is sometimes not painless.

Tom and Cathy have a curious, combative relationship. They remind me of Maddie and David on *Moonlighting*. They're always teasing and fighting, but it's obvious there's something there. As uninvolved and attractive people, it's surprising that they haven't at least tried going out together. But who am I to say? I thought Sonny and Cher were perfect for each other.

After breakfast, Cathy returns to her office to catch up on paperwork. She is the consummate Canadian success story. In grade 13, her average was 92 percent. Both Carleton and Western offered her generous scholarships. She decided that Western was perfect. It was close to Sarnia, and had a prestigious school of medicine. My parents were calling her Doctor Richardson before we'd even left high school.

However, not only did Cathy not become a doctor, she didn't even go on to post-secondary education.

Knowing that her scholarship would cover most of her expenses, she felt no sense of urgency to get a summer job. Therefore, in the summer of grade 13, while I slaved at the refinery, sis opened her own business. Combining her artistic flair with her love of horticulture, she founded Richardson Landscaping. The corporate name was simple, but the concept was pure genius.

Cathy spent the first four weeks of the summer combing the nicer neighbourhoods in Sarnia. When she spotted a property that she felt would look better if landscaped differently, she would do a series of sketches until she perfected *the look*. While basking in the sun at the beach, she would do a water colour of the final sketch.

The young entrepreneur would then frame the painting herself, tastefully, of course. A sticker on the back simply read, *This is how Richardson Landscaping sees your home.* The framed picture was delivered, via courier, to the homeowner. The total cost to Cathy was approximately fifty dollars per picture.

Over the course of four weeks, she completed seventeen of these impressive and unique *business cards.* At the end of the month, Cathy started following up with phone calls and she booked an amazing fifteen appointments.

At this point, I was still far from impressed. Four weeks into the summer, Cathy's venture was eight hundred and fifty dollars in debt, and I was constantly lending her money. As far as I knew, her scholarship did not include an honorarium to repay her brother.

Within a few days, though, I was no longer worried. I was jealous!

Cathy's pitch at the appointments was, to use my students' favourite word, "awesome." For a flat fee of one thousand dollars, she offered to gather tenders from four local landscaping firms, hire the appropriate choice, oversee all activities, and ensure that the job came in on time and on budget. There was no charge for her design.

Cathy's contagious enthusiasm, sound business proposal, and beautiful designs netted her six of the fifteen potential clients.Eleven years ago, six thousand dollars was an unbelievable summer job!

She spent the rest of July and August supervising the six projects. Every customer was thrilled with the end result. Because she stayed on top of the landscaping companies, jobs actually came in at prices substantially under the norm. In essence, her services paid for themselves.

Referrals started pouring in and she has never looked back. Last year, working only eight months, she made more money than my father and I combined.

At first, it was difficult to accept the fact that my sister, a university dropout before she even got there, was *a mover and a shaker.* However, when I saw the type of Christmas and birthday gifts that success translated into, I became fiercely proud of her.

Despite her great achievement, Cathy is still a one-woman operation, preferring to handle all typing, billing, accounts payable and other clerical duties herself – Saturdays.

That's all right with Tom and me, because she wouldn't accompany us for the next item on our Saturday-in-Sarnia agenda, anyway. We go to the barber. It is one of the high points of the weekend. I'm sure most people don't think of a trip to the barber as a high point but, then again, most people don't get their hair cut at Miller's Barber Shop.

Roy Miller started giving us *buzz cuts* when we were five years old. We've outgrown that style, but remained true to Roy. In addition to being a very intelligent and witty fellow, he has the one quality that most endears a man to Tom and to me – he's a die-hard Tiger fan!

Like most barbers, Roy has a few Saturday regulars who are there only to pass the time. Two of the three, Jimmy and Clyde, don't have any hair left to cut. Clyde, in particular, gets a real kick out of our monthly visits. He is a big baseball fan, too – if you can be and cheer for the Blue Jays.

During the warm-weather months, the next item on Tom's and my itinerary is golfing. Both of us love the game but, despite being reasonably good athletes who have played golf for several years, neither of us excels at the sport. I have a fifteen handicap, while Tom's fluctuates between sixteen and twenty-two, depending on who's asking.

Saturday nights in Sarnia hold something different each month. Sometimes we assemble for a house party or a ballgame. But most frequently, ten or fifteen of us descend upon JB's, a popular local bar with an outdoor patio overlooking a marina.

Sundays, Sue and I go to church and out to brunch with her parents, whom I enjoy immensely. The Washburns have done quite well for themselves, owning and operating an industrial cleaning company. Like so many others, the company fell upon tough times in the early eighties. Unlike so many others, due in large part to my in-laws' work ethic and a debt-free balance sheet, it weathered the storm.

I wouldn't call them rich, but well-to-do wouldn't be pushing it. They have a new home on the lake, a cottage, a boat, and two nice cars. I don't think they have much in the way of investment assets, but with no debt, good cash flow and a saleable business, their financial worries seem to be nonexistent.

After Sunday brunch, Sue and I head back to Kitchener. On the way out of town, we stop at Heaven's Gate Nursing Home. I still can't believe they named it that. Our only living grandparent, my grandmother, has been *waiting at the gate* for five years now. The doctors claim she is in excellent mental health, but I fear otherwise. She has developed the alarming habit of cheering for the Blue Jays.

Finally, we arrive back in Kitchener, and spend Sunday evening recovering from the hectic weekend.

However, this upcoming weekend, our once-a-month routine will be slightly altered. On Friday, instead of going out after dinner, Sue and I are staying at my parents' so I can talk to my father. When I phoned him yesterday, I simply said that I needed to talk to him. I did not go into any details.

What a mistake! Mom called back five minutes later in hysterics. "Are Susan and the baby all right?" she demanded. "Are you all right? Did Cathy tell you something she hasn't told us? Are –"

To prevent my mother's impending coronary, I interrupted her barrage of questions and told her what I wanted to talk to Dad about– our finances.

Did it help? No. My mother persisted.

"Do you need money?" she continued shrilly. "Are you in trouble? Does this have to do with the time you–"

"No, Mom! I just need some basic financial planning advice."

"What led to this after all these years?" she asked skeptically. "What are you hiding from me?"

The fact is that when it comes to finances, I have nothing to hide. My lack of financial knowledge had really hit me for the first time just the other day. I was reading a local business publication when I stumbled across a *Self-Analysis Financial Planning Test.*

No sweat, I thought. I'm a teacher. I don't fail tests; I fail students. Confidently, I picked up my pencil and set about responding to questions such as these:

- Have you selected the proper amortization period for your mortage?
- Is your will up-to-date?
- Could your dependents live comfortably in the event of your death?
- If you plan to retire early, have you set up a suitable savings program?

- How do you plan to pay for your children's education?
- Fifty percent of Canadians retire in financial hardship. What are you doing to guarantee you won't be one of them?
- Are your debts structured properly?

Not only could I not give a satisfactory answer to many of the questions, I didn't even understand some of them. I caught an ominous glimpse of Susan, our sons and me living as bag people.

I dropped my pencil, an unnerved man. It's not that I want to be a multimillionaire although, like everyone else, I do. I'll settle for being comfortable – very comfortable. I'd like to own a nice home and a cottage, help my children get an education, and retire in relative affluence at a reasonable age. And I want to accomplish all of this without substantially sacrificing my present standard of living.

I think these goals are shared by most Canadians. Are they realistic? Can they be realized on an average salary? If so, how?

Within an hour of reading that article, I was committed to learning the basics of financial planning. I had no desire to learn the intricacies of the stock market, nor was it my goal to be able to recite mortgage tables from memory.

All I wanted to know was how best to get where I want to be from where I am now.

I figured Dad is no financial genius, but he must have learned a few things in his fifty-eight years. He seemed as good a place as any to start.

|2|
A SURPRISING
REFERRAL

That April weekend trip to Sarnia changed my life.

* * * * *

The smell of my father's cigar, the voices of the Tiger radio
announcers and talks about saving money rather than spending it do not rank high on Sue's list of favourite things. Throwing them all together proved to be too much for her. Claiming
fatigue, she retired early that Friday night. My mother also
bade us farewell – not to sleep, however, but to tackle the
monthly chore of paying the bills.

Dad and I sat down to talk about something that, in our
twenty-eight years together, we had never discussed before.
In these days of open conversations about everything, including sexual habits, money remains a relatively taboo subject,
even among family members. When you think about that, it's
amazing!

"I can't believe we've never talked about money before," I
marvelled.

"Even if we had, it would have been a short conversation,"
replied Dad. "Up until five years ago, I didn't know a thing
about finances. Your mother and I lived from pay-cheque to
pay-cheque, making our mortgage payments, staying out of
debt, and sometimes saving for things we wanted. The only
thing your grandparents really told me about money management was not to borrow.

"We couldn't teach you what we didn't know, and your
grandparents couldn't teach us what they didn't know. I don't
think it's our fault as a family. I suspect most people have the
same problem, and I blame it partly on our education system.

"Five years ago, when I finally learned the basics of financial planning, I couldn't believe how straightforward they were. It's just common sense. If I had looked into the fundamentals thirty years ago, or even fifteen years ago, your mother and I would be very well-off today."

"And I'd love you even more than I do now," I interjected. "But Dad, for someone who didn't know much, you seem to have done all right."

"All right," he echoed, "but not great. And the frustrating part is that I now know great is achievable...easily achievable. It's incomprehensible to me that our government has not altered school curriculum to include a basic family finance course. All high school graduates should know how to fill out an income-tax form properly. They should know how to select their mortgage, how to finance their children's education, and how to save and plan for retirement.

"You know me, David. I've always believed that our country's education system is second to none, but that doesn't mean it can't use some improvement. There's no debating the fact that one of the most crucial improvements would be to teach basic money skills. Hell, we're raising generation after generation of financial illiterates. I don't think that even the politicians understand the tremendous benefits the economy would enjoy if Joe Average knew how to handle his money properly."

"Dad, why did you –"

"I can't believe Sparky is leaving Jack Morris in the game," Dad interrupted. "They're pounding him!" he added, as he rose to put the dog out.

As Dad left the room, I realized just how right he was. Sparky should have taken Morris out.

He was also right about most Canadians being financial illiterates.There is no excuse for us possessing as little financial knowledge as we do. When even a university-educated person like me is embarrassed by an elementary financial test, something is wrong. Although I'd never thought about it before, Dad was also right about the fault lying with our education system. I teach history and geography, but I have to admit that being able to date the Battle of Hastings at 1066 A.D. is of little consequence compared to being able to create a proper savings program. Both forms of knowledge are important, and a balance must be found.

Dad re-entered the room to a Jack Morris game-ending

strikeout. "Boy, is he a clutch pitcher, a great competitor," he beamed. "Big win, big win."

"How did you even manage to do 'all right' without knowing anything?" I continued.

"I'm not sure I like the way you phrased that," Dad laughed. "I brought home a fairly good income and we didn't have an extravagant lifestyle. God knows you never wanted for anything, but we had no investment assets at all. Often, we didn't have any more than a couple of hundred dollars in the bank.

"Our only hard-and-fast rule was not to borrow. If we needed a new car, wanted to go on a trip, or had to put a new roof on the house, we would save the money first. If we didn't have anything specific on our *wish list*, we spent our entire monthly income. That was our complete *financial plan*, so to speak."

"You borrowed to buy the house, though?"

"Oh, yes, obviously, we had to borrow to buy the house. The trust company gave us a twenty-five year mortgage that we finished paying off five years ago," Dad answered. "Actually, five years ago, a lot of things came together. We made our final mortgage payment. You were graduating and, except for not being able to make your own bed and cook, you were becoming self-sufficient. Our income increased significantly through my textbook sales, and your uncle died and left your mother twenty-five thousand dollars."

"I didn't know that!" I exclaimed, surprised.

"You were at the funeral," Dad laughed.

"No, no, not that Uncle George died. That he left Mom twenty-five thousand dollars."

"We wanted to surprise you by leaving you more than just the house. You know, something to help you get over the inevitable trauma of losing the two greatest influences on your life."

"Yeah, yeah," I said, rolling my eyes.

"Anyway, when all those things happened at once, it became painfully obvious that I needed some financial advice. We had a couple of thousand dollars a month to play with and almost twenty-seven thousand sitting in the bank. I was ten years from retirement and both your mother and I figured we'd better seek professional help.

"I just didn't want to do something stupid. I knew that with my pension plan, my retirement looked pretty good. But I also knew that if I handled our new-found nest egg and our monthly surplus funds well, your mother and I could be looking at a cottage, a boat, some trips, or maybe even all of these. Both of us had always wanted a place on the lake and this was our chance."

"So, what did you do? Something intelligent I hope, considering that someday all this could be mine."

"What about your sister? Don't you think it's only fair to leave her half?"

"Jackie Onassis? C'mon, Dad, it's pocket change for her," I joked. "Seriously, what did you do?"

"I got the best haircut of my life," he deadpanned.

"Get serious, Dad. I really –"

"I am serious. I was down at Roy's one Saturday and I started talking to James Murray. You know James... He's always there on Saturdays with Clyde and Jimmy."

"I know him well."

"Well, what you probably don't know is that before he became so successful selling real estate, he did stints as both a stockbroker and a life insurance agent. I told him I was in the market for some financial planning advice and asked him if he could recommend anyone.Even though he had been out of the field for about ten years, I figured he would still know someone competent.

"He smiled and said, 'The best financial planner in town is holding a razor at your throat.' "

"Roy? C'mon," I said, disbelieving.

"I'm not kidding and neither was James. Over the next several months, as he cut my hair, Roy taught me the basics of financial planning. And you'll be pleased to hear that right now my finances are in great shape, and they're looking better all the time."

"You're right. I am pleased to hear that. But how the heck does a barber become a financial planning expert?"

"The answer to that, in fact Roy's background in general, is quite interesting. As you know, Roy and I were high school classmates. He was the all-American Canadian boy. You know what I mean...good-looking, athletic, bright, funny. Everybody liked Roy. He was our class valedictorian and was voted most likely to succeed.

"He had always talked about being a lawyer, so naturally he was Western-bound as a first step."

"There are other universities, Dad," I interrupted.

"Only in your mind, son. Anyway, Roy and I lived in the same residence at university, but I didn't see him much. Between studying, playing varsity basketball and coming home to visit his girl friend, he was a busy guy.

"In second year, five of us, including Roy, decided to rent a house. The first month was unbelievable. You know how it is. You aren't far enough into the courses to have papers or midterms, so you party every night. Remember all the things I told you not to do at university? Well, I was speaking from experience.

"Then, one night in early October, Roy got a phone call saying his father had died of a heart attack. By the next afternoon he had dropped out of school and moved back to Sarnia.

"His father, a fine man, had a history of heart problems. He had only worked at the refinery for ten years when he had his first heart attack. The doctors told him not to go back to physical work but, unfortunately, he wasn't qualified for much else. To his credit, he didn't give up. Instead, he trained to become a barber and eventually opened Miller's barbershop.

"Mrs. Miller worked as a maid during the day and as a waitress at night. Neither of them made a lot of money, but together they had enough to get by.

"When Mr. Miller died, Roy felt he had no choice but to quit school and go home to work. There was no way Mrs. Miller and Roy's younger sister, Ellen, could survive on a maid's pay. And, like so many people, Mr. Miller didn't carry enough life insurance.

"During high school, Roy had become a pretty darn good barber himself. He had learned the tricks of the trade from hanging around his father's shop. When his dad was really busy, Roy would cut hair to help out. In fact, in our first year at university, he cut hair in residence to make some extra money.

"When Roy had to return home from university, his game plan was simple. He was going to operate the barbershop until Ellen had completed college, and then he was going to sell it and go back to school. His sister was only in grade eleven at the time, so he was looking at about six years.

"We all felt badly about Roy having to put off his dream of becoming a lawyer, but deep down we knew he was doing the right thing. You've got to be there when your family needs you, even if it means personal sacrifice. You would do well to remember that, son, when your mother and I are old and want to move in with you."

"Don't even joke about that," I laughed. "You still haven't explained how Roy became a financial planning expert. This isn't going to be one of your famous three-hour stories, is it?"

"No, no. I'm getting to the financial part.

"Roy did a tremendous job running the barbershop. He did some things that, at the time, were unique. Without a doubt, the most innovative and profitable was *the hair truck.* Apart from the Tigers, Roy has always had two main hobbies. One is going to auctions and the other is tinkering with old cars and trucks. In his second year at the shop, he combined the two hobbies beautifully.

"He bought a barber chair at an auction and installed it in the back of an old moving truck. Then, he put in a basin complete with running water, a power supply, and even a magazine rack. On Tuesdays, Roy took the hair truck to the refineries. He lifted the sliding door on the back and, voilà, he was open for business. The workers flocked over during their breaks and lunches... It was so convenient. What was the worst day of the week for most barbers was now Roy's best. In fact, he did so well on Tuesdays, he hired another barber to go back on Wednesdays and Thursdays. Eventually, a new by-law put a stop to all the fun. But in the four or five years the hair truck was in operation, Roy brought in a lot of business and, more importantly, built a large and loyal clientele.

"He wasn't making a corporate lawyer's wage, but he was doing well...very well. We've never discussed what we make, but I would think our incomes over the years have been quite similar."

"What happened to the six-year plan?" I asked.

"Roy loved being a barber. It's as simple as that. To this day, he loves working downtown, dealing with people, owning his own business, all of it. It's funny, but Roy has really lived up to his most-likely-to-succeed billing. I don't know a more successful, well-rounded person."

"What about the financial planning part, Dad? I have to be home by Sunday, you know."

"I'm getting there. I'm getting there. Roy was really shaken by the poor financial shape his mother had been left in. His father had had no pension, no savings, and very little insurance. Roy laughs now when he says the only thing his father left them was a mortgage, but it wasn't funny at the time.

"He vowed not to make the same mistakes. Yet, after a couple of years running the shop and making a good income, Roy had very little to show for his efforts. His mother and sister were being well taken care of but, financially, that was about it.

"Roy decided it was time to do something. He started reading everything he could on money management. At that time, almost all financial books concentrated on investment alternatives, not on mundane topics like saving, buying a house, and insurance; you know, the common person's concerns. They all showed what to do with money once you had it, but they didn't tell you how to accumulate it.

"However, Roy's father had always told him that if you want to learn to do something right, watch someone who does it successfully. Roy reasoned that that certainly held true for sports, so it probably held true for just about everything else too, including financial planning.

"So, at the age of twenty-three, Roy did what he now calls the smartest thing he has ever done. He went to visit Maurice White.

"Old Mr. White was one of the wealthiest men in town. He owned a jewelry store, a huge farm, several race horses and half the real estate downtown. Included in those holdings was the building that housed Miller's barbershop.

"Mr. White had always liked Roy. He admired him for his loyalty to his family and he was also quite impressed with Roy's entrepreneurial approach to increasing business. When Roy told Mr. White why he had dropped by, Mr. White nodded, 'You've come to the right place, my lad. I'll teach you *the golden secret* of financial success in one hour.'

"Well, David, that was quite an hour. I venture to say there aren't many barbers who started with nothing and today own a beautiful house on the lake, a large investment portfolio, an office building, and have their retirement well taken care of."

"All that from just one secret? What was it?" I asked eagerly.

"Slow down. It's not that simple. Roy continued to read and learn about financial planning. His knowledge of insurance, RRSPs and investments has really helped him. But there's no doubt that hour was the catalyst. I'm not telling you any more, though. Roy teaches financial planning better than anyone, and I know he'll be more than happy to share his knowledge with you. In fact, I've already told him you won't just be talking about the Tigers tomorrow."

"I'm not sure I'll be able to follow him," I worried. "I don't understand all those fancy money terms and, as you may remember, math was never my strong suit."

"As I said earlier, son, it's just common sense. You'll be astonished when you learn how easy it is to handle your finances properly. If you listen to Roy, you'll never have any financial worries. You'll be so wealthy you'll be able to build your mother and me a guest house down in Kitchener."

"I'm not sure I want to be wealthy after all," I smiled.

* * * * *

"Boy, are you tanned!" I complimented Cathy, over breakfast. "It's only April and you're mahogany."

"Hanging out at the tanning studios?" Tom asked. "Man, that's an expensive habit. How much do those sessions cost?"

"Well, uh, I haven't been going to the studios. I bought my own tanning machine," an embarrassed Cathy replied.

"Must be nice! I slave all day at the plant to make ends meet and you're buying your own electric beach! If you'd just work on your personality a bit, I'd ask you to marry me."

"What if one of the girls you asked last night at the bar says yes? Bigamy is illegal, you know, Tom," Cathy pointed out.

"Oh, Tom," I groaned, "you weren't using that stale line again? What happened to, 'Excuse me, miss, can I buy you a Porsche?' "

"Gimme a break, you two! To meet women, a man has gotta do what a man has gotta do. Besides, that Porsche line has served me pretty well over the years."

"Well, I think it's running out of gas," Cathy teased.

"Did you really buy a tanning machine, sis?"

"Yeah. I had some extra money and I love being dark. Besides, it didn't cost all that much."

"I bet," I said sarcastically. "What do you do with all your money? You must own half of Sarnia by now."

"Hardly. Between my car payments, mortgage payments, condo fees, credit cards and daily living expenses, there's hardly anything left."

"Tough life, baby," Tom sighed. "You really should apply for some sort of government aid. SISIM or something – Supplemental Income for Single Independent Millionairesses."

"How can you party so hard last night and still be so witty in the morning, Tom? It never ceases to amaze me. Anyway, the truth is, I've blown my money pretty badly. Except for my down payment, my furnishings and a small RRSP, I haven't saved much at all. I get calls all the time from brokers and insurance agents who want to give me advice, but I distrust insurance agents, and I don't understand a thing brokers say."

"Talk about perfect timing. You won't believe the conversation I had with Dad last night! That's why I didn't go out. I wanted to discuss financial planning. With Sue and I about to have a baby, I want to start investigating things. We're looking for a house now; I'll need insurance; a college education fund for Davey Junior – all that stuff."

"Davey Junior? You must be kidding," Tom cracked, in between mouthfuls of his tenth piece of toast.

"So, what did Dad say? I didn't know he knew anything about money."

"He didn't until five years ago. Then he learned the basics of financial planning and now he says he's in great shape. I'll tell you something. You guys won't believe who taught him – Roy Miller."

"What the hell does Roy know about financial planning?" Tom demanded.

"A lot. You know how we figured Roy's wife must have inherited some pretty big money? Uh, uh. It turns out the house, the BMW, the boat, everything – all earned through good financial planning. Roy started from scratch and, with only average earnings, turned himself into one wealthy barber."

"How?"

"I don't know yet, but you can bet I'm going to find out. In fact, our favourite barber is going to start teaching me this morning. Dad says Roy will teach me all I need to know to gain financial peace of mind."

"That sounds great. Do you two mind if I tag along today?" Cathy asked hopefully. "I don't need a shave – but I do need the advice."

"No, come on along," I invited her. "Who knows? Maybe one Saturday years from now, we'll be eating brunch on the Mediterranean, remembering this as the most important morning of our lives."

"The wealthy barber," Tom muttered, shaking his head.

|3|
THE WEALTHY
BARBER

When we arrived at Roy's, he was just finishing up Mr. Thacker's shave, if you can call it a shave. I don't think Mr. Thacker has had any facial hair growth since he turned ninety, five years ago.

"How are you, Johnny?" Mr. Thacker inquired, looking me straight in the eye.

"I'm Dave."

"Sorry, Dan. I always get you confused with your brother."

"I don't have a brother, Mr. Thacker. You're thinking of – "

"Dear me, what happened to your brother? The poor boy couldn't have been more than thirty!"

"I never had a brother. You're thinking of – "

"Oh, yes, I'm sorry. I thought you were one of the Richardson boys, the principal's sons."

I wasn't at all sure how to proceed at this point, but before I had a chance to decide, Mr. Thacker had started for the door.

"The old boy's getting a bit senile, eh, Roy?" I sympathized, after the door had closed.

"Are you kidding, Davey? He knew who you were the whole time. It's all an act. He figures I won't ask him to pay if I think he's losing it."

"So, do you make him pay?" asked Tom.

"Sure do. If I gave a free cut to every weirdo who came in, I'd be broke in a month, and you two boys wouldn't have paid in years.

"Nice tan, Cathy!" Roy commented, before returning his attention to me. "Hey, Dave, did you see the article in the *Observer* last Wednesday on the female Donald Trump here?"

Roy was referring to a full-page feature in the local paper

that made my sister sound like the smartest and most talented woman alive.

"My mother showed it to me," I answered. "Five times."

"If you want to make it six, it's on the bottom of my birdcage," Tom injected with a chuckle.

I myself didn't find that line particularly funny, but it got a couple of knee-slaps from Jimmy, who was reading the paper in the corner.

"Hey, where's Clyde?" I wondered.

"He's on holidays," James Murray informed me, "down in Florida at his sister's. I heard it was ninety-eight degrees down there yesterday. He'll be on a liquid diet for sure."

At this point I hopped up into Roy's chair. I always go before Tom, who insists on making sure Roy is *on* before he'll go near him.

"I was talking to my father last night about financial planning. With Sue and I about to buy a house and have a baby, I figured it's time I learn a few things. Dad told me you know more about financial planning than anybody, so Cathy, Tom and I are hoping you can teach us the basics."

"Your father mentioned on Thursday that he was going to recommend you talk to me. Like I told him, I'd be more than happy to help out. He came to see me five years ago himself, and we put him on the right track."

"So I heard. That's good news. But he had some money to invest. I'm not sure you'll be able to do much for me. The only money Sue and I have is what we've saved for our down payment."

"Dave, investing and financial planning are not synonymous. Financial planning is really nothing more than the proper handling of cash flow and assets to meet your objectives. Oh, there are wills and insurance and a few other things, and we'll talk about all that later, but, basically, how you handle your income and assets will determine your success.

"Let's be honest. Most young people don't have any assets, except maybe a home. So, it comes down to managing your cash flow."

"You mean budgeting?" I queried. "I'm terrible at that."

"No, I don't mean budgeting. Everybody's terrible at that. Very few people have become financially successful through budgeting, and the ones who have aren't much fun at parties."

"Ho, ho," Cathy piped up. "So, if we don't budget, how do

we save money? I sure never have any left at the end of the month. I spend everything. The better business gets, the more I spend."

"Let's not get ahead of ourselves here. I admire your enthusiasm, but let's slow down a bit.

"I can make all three of you financially successful. I've done it for lots of people, these clowns included," Roy said, nodding at Jimmy and James. "Starting next month, each time you come in, I'll teach you a different part of a solid financial plan. Seven months from now, you'll be on the road to prosperity, and you'll tell everyone that Roy Miller is the greatest man who ever lived."

"We already tell people that, Roy," smiled Tom.

"How can you teach us so much in so little time? I mean, Roy, you really are working with novices. Tom and Dave and I are financial idiots!"

"Cathy, my job will be removing the word 'financial' from that statement. You'll have to worry about the other part yourselves. Trust me... Good financial planning is nothing more than common sense. The old KISS philosophy at its best. Keep It Simple...Sarnians.

"We all share pretty much the same goals – an annual vacation, a nice car, a comfortable home, a cottage, early retirement, the ability to give our children what they need and want ...and baseball season's tickets. These are the average Canadian's goals.

"And I'll tell you right now, they're easily attainable...easily. Especially if you start young. Time is your greatest ally. If you three start now, I guarantee you that you will exceed all your goals – dramatically.

"Look at me. I'm a barber, for crying out loud! I'm proud of my business, but I'm the first to admit that I'm not pulling in a doctor's salary. Far from it. Yet you'd be hard-pressed to find many professionals with better financial statements than mine. I hope it doesn't sound like I'm bragging. It's just that it's important for you to know that if someone as simple as me can become wealthy, it's certainly possible for you geniuses."

"You're not simple, Roy. Maybe a bit slow, but not simple," cracked Tom.

"I don't want to seem cynical, Roy, but if it's so easy, why isn't everyone doing it?" I asked.

"Lack of knowledge. Your dad and I talk about this all the

time. Our schools don't teach money skills. Our family members don't talk money. And, just as importantly, there are very few places for an aspiring learner to turn. Our financial industry is geared toward product sales, not toward dispensing well-rounded financial planning advice.

"Most insurance agents sell cash-value policies; mutual fund salespeople sell funds and tax shelters; brokers sell stocks and bonds; bankers sell guaranteed investment certificates, and so on and so on. You can't blame them. Product sales are where the money is, so very few of them are true *financial planners.*"

"Are there any good product-oriented financial planners?" I asked.

"Sure there are, but none can do as well for you as you can do for yourself if you're well-informed."

Tom looked quizzical. "What about *fee-only* planners?"

"Don't depend too much on financial planners," Roy replied emphatically. "Learn for yourself. Nobody cares as much about your money as you do. You have to take responsibility for your own future. As I said earlier, the great thing is, it's not hard."

"Dad said last night that some old guy taught you a golden secret when you were young. What is it?" I probed.

"Oh, no. I'm saving that for next month. If you only pay attention once in the next seven months, let it be next month. If you follow that lesson, even if you do everything else poorly, I guarantee you – someday you'll be rich."

"Can't we start today?" I implored.

"No," to my chagrin, was his firm answer. "My granddaughter's going to be here in five minutes. I'm taking care of her for the afternoon. Cathy can stay, but I want you two out of here ASAP. At three years old, I don't want to scare Emily off men for the rest of her life."

Never before had I been tempted to get my hair cut two consecutive weeks. Roy had really piqued my interest. I've known him all my life and he has always come across as a very modest man. The matter-of-fact confidence he displayed when discussing Tom's, Cathy's and my financial futures was out of character – and contagious. There was no doubt in my mind that I had taken the first step along the road to financial prosperity.

4
THE TEN PERCENT
SOLUTION

I can't remember a rainstorm worse than the one that occurred on the third Saturday in May. A north wind had come up and was blowing at seventy kilometers an hour. That, combined with a torrential downpour, had caused most Sarnians to stay inside. Most smart Sarnians, that is.

There was no way Tom, Cathy and I were going to miss out on the golden secret. We had been looking forward to it for a month. We were so excited, we even skipped breakfast at the Chalet.

As usual, I drove. My parents' house has indoor access to the garage and both Tom and Cathy have underground parking so, surprisingly, it was possible to remain perfectly dry until we arrived at the shop. On the way there, Cathy suggested that Roy might be closed because of the weather. Tom and I just laughed. Roy hasn't missed an entire day of work in thirty-seven years for any reason. He had even opened on the morning of his daughter's wedding.

With so few people venturing out, we were able to get the parking spot right in front of Miller's. Between our umbrellas and his awning, we managed to get from the car to the shop door relatively unscathed.

It was locked.

Clyde, with his Florida tan, was standing on the other side peering out through the glass. "All you have to do is say, 'We love the Blue Jays,' and I'll let you in. We've got coffee brewing," he chirped in his reedy voice.

By this time, we were starting to get pretty wet. And annoyed. The angle of the rain was such that it was impossible to protect yourself completely, even with the help of the awning and umbrellas.

"I love the Blue Jays!" Cathy cried, not amused.

Traitor. Tom and I stood stoically.

Clyde shook his head and let all of us in. "You boys really are die-hards. You should seek professional help."

"You telling us we need a psychiatrist is like Karl Malden telling someone she needs a nose job," Tom murmured, as he towelled off.

"I thought you three might not show. It's terrible out there," Roy commented.

"What? And miss our long-awaited, eagerly anticipated first lesson? You've got to be kidding!" I retorted. "What I can't believe is that these three have shown up in this weather," I added, motioning toward Clyde, Jimmy, and James Murray. I'm not sure why I always use James Murray's given and family names. Perhaps it's because, when I was young, I thought his name was James-Murray, like Billy-Bob or Bobby-Joe.

"They wouldn't miss free coffee and doughnuts if we had a tornado. You should know that by now," Roy replied, as he straightened up the counter.

"Roy, I've been looking forward to today for a month. My financial situation is getting worse instead of better," Cathy began impatiently. "I can hardly wait to hear what you have to say."

"Okay, let's get started. As your father has probably told you, I took over this shop thirty-odd years ago when my dad died. I got lucky and a few of my ideas paid off. After a couple of years, I was making a pretty good income. Very good for a barber. I added a couple of chairs in the other room and, all in all, things were moving along well.

"I decided to make barbering my life's work. I knew my income from the shop was respectable, but it was never going to make me a rich man. That bothered me because, frankly, I wanted to be wealthy. I grew up poor and, believe me, it's something you don't acquire a taste for. I didn't want to live in town in a tiny, one-bedroom home – I wanted to live on the lake. I wanted to own this building, too. I wanted a nice car, trips to Europe and some of the other fine things life has to offer.

"The only way I could accomplish all that on my income was to budget and save like a madman. Or, at least, that's what I thought. So, I developed a budget...so much for rent, so much for food, so much for clothes, so much for savings...you know.

Two years after starting to budget, I had very little to show for it. Sure enough, at the end of each month I'd end up saying, 'So much for savings,' but, unfortunately, it didn't mean what I had hoped it would mean. It was pretty depressing.

"Like you, Dave, I realized I didn't know anything about financial planning, and it was high time to learn. I didn't have a father to turn to, so I went to a person who I figured must know a lot about money, he had so much – Old Mr. White.

"I explained my situation to him. I told him what I wanted to achieve. 'Is it possible?' I asked.

"He told me, 'Wealth beyond your wildest dreams is possible if you follow the golden rule: Invest ten percent of all you make for long-term growth. If you follow that one simple guideline, someday you'll be a very rich man.' "

"That's it?" asked Tom. "I could have gotten that from a Bank of Nova Scotia commercial!"

"Patience, Tom," replied Roy. "Patience. I felt the same way myself. I wasn't very impressed when Mr. White told me, either. My budget was already designed to save even more than ten percent and, at that point, it wasn't working and I was far from wealthy. But Mr. White went on to explain a few things that I'll tell you now...things that turn a seemingly simple sentence into an extremely powerful thought.

"Cathy, if you invested twenty-four hundred dollars a year, say two hundred dollars a month, for the next thirty years, and averaged a fifteen percent return a year, how much money do you think you'd end up with?" challenged Roy.

"Well, twenty-four hundred times thirty is...seventy-two thousand – "

"I'm impressed," I interrupted.

"...plus growth... I don't know... I'd say two hundred thousand. Maybe not quite that much," Cathy concluded.

"Wrong. The answer is one point four million dollars," Roy declared.

"Get real!" was Tom's initial reaction. When he realized that Roy was serious, he paled. "What about inflation? And where am I going to get fifteen percent? For that matter, where am I going to get two hundred dollars a month?" he stammered.

"All good questions, Tom, and we'll get to them in due course. Dave, you try one. If you had started putting thirty dollars a month away, the equivalent of a dollar a day, at age eighteen and you continued until age sixty-five, averaging a fifteen percent annual return, how much would you end up with?"

"I hate math, Roy, but I'll give it a shot. Thirty dollars a month is three hundred and sixty dollars a year, times forty-seven years... Anybody have a calculator?"

"It's just under seventeen thousand," injected Roy.

"Plus growth. I'll say around seventy thousand."

"Close," responded Roy. "The answer is two million six hundred and seventy-nine thousand dollars."

"Bull," scoffed Tom, as if he had read my mind.

"No, not bull...magic. The magic of compound interest. The eighth wonder of the world. Thirty dollars a month, a dollar a day, will magically turn into over two and a half million. And do you know what's even more impressive? You know someone who has done it," Roy said proudly.

"Thirty-five years ago, I started my savings with thirty dollars a month, which was approximately ten percent of my earnings. I have achieved a fifteen percent average annual return, actually a little higher. In addition, as my income rose, my ten percent saving component rose accordingly. Thirty dollars a month became sixty dollars, then a hundred, and eventually hundreds of dollars a month.

"You three are looking at a very wealthy man."

"Are you trying to tell us that, by saving ten percent of every pay-cheque, you've turned yourself into a millionaire?" an intense Tom demanded.

"Precisely," was the incredible response.

Roy Miller, a millionaire! I sat stunned. I knew he had done well, but a millionaire? To the best of my knowledge, I'd never met a millionaire, and I sure didn't expect my first to be my barber. Roy was clearly deriving great pleasure from the disbelief on our three faces.

"Compound interest...mind-boggling, isn't it?" he went on. "When the Indians sold Manhattan to the Dutch for beads worth twenty-four dollars, it seemed like the natives got taken. But, if they had invested that money at eight percent interest, today their tribe would be worth over eleven trillion dollars."

"Have you ever thought about buying Manhattan, Roy?" Cathy teased.

"It's a real tragedy that most people don't understand compound interest and its wondrous powers. Take your dad, David. If he had started his program at the same time I did, you'd be looking at a big inheritance down the road."

"You still haven't answered my questions about the effects of inflation, where we get fifteen percent, and how we save two hundred a month. Hell, I'm lucky to save two hundred a year and, even if I could save money, I don't know anything about investing – the stock market, options, commodities... C'mon, Roy, you've got to be kidding!"

Tom's points were well taken. Saving money is never easy. No one – and I mean no one – has devoted more time to developing a budget than Susan and I. Yet every month, apart from our down-payment fund, we don't manage to save a cent. As for investing, the only investment I've ever made was a stock on the Vancouver exchange. I lost a thousand dollars in one week. A thousand dollars I couldn't afford to lose. A thousand dollars that was needed for my tuition.

"I'll talk about saving and investing in a minute," Roy commenced. "As for inflation, well, I'm sure that, in the mid-fifties, people probably said, 'Yeah, saving ten percent sounds like a good idea, but what's a couple of million going to be worth in the eighties, anyway?' Sure, inflation is going to have an impact. But not a devastating one. Far from it. In fact, inflation is all the more reason to save. Things are going to get more expensive. Lakefront properties are going to continue to rise in price. Jaguars are going to cost more. But, believe me, if you save ten percent, you'll be parking your XJ6 beside your cottage someday. Remember that your wages will continue to rise too, as will your ten percent saving. My original ten percent stake was only thirty dollars a month; yours will be much more, and so will your total wealth. That will do a lot to offset inflation. If you handle your savings wisely, your growth rate should far exceed the inflation rate. Maybe not every year, but certainly on average.

"It's the person who doesn't save ten percent who has to worry about inflation, not the person who does," he summarized.

"So how do we earn fif –"

"Slow down, slow down. Let's talk about saving the money first. When people think about saving, they think about budgeting. I'll allot so much of my income for this, so much for that, et cetera, et cetera, and at the end of the month, I'll have so much left over. But as each of us knows all too well, something goes wrong. Money keeps running out before the month does.

"You know, it's funny. When I took over the shop, it was obvious that cost management hadn't been one of my father's strengths. I designed a detailed budget that covered all my potential expenses. I stuck to it like glue. That budget played a major part in my early success. To this day, I still do a shop budget once a year. And I still stick to it.

"After a couple of years running the shop, I couldn't understand how my personal budget could be such a waste of time, while my business budget worked like a charm. I discussed the situation with Old Mr. White. I'll never forget his reply. 'Roy, my young friend,' he said, 'a business only has to budget for needs. It's in the best interest of the business to limit those needs as much as possible. An individual, on the other hand, must budget for both needs and wants. It is a rare person who can do that successfully because, for too many people, **a want becomes a need.**'

"And it's so true! Did I need a new car in my second year of business, or did I just want one? Cathy, did you need to get away to Europe last winter, or did you just want to? Tom, did you need, or just want, the best stereo available? It's human nature to spend our entire disposable income and to rationalize all those expenditures as needs."

"Good point, Roy, but you have to have some fun, too. One of the reasons I make money is to spend it on things I like," I argued.

"Young people of all generations think alike, Dave. That's exactly what I said to Mr. White. Remember, I grew up poor. My first couple of years at the shop was the first time I'd ever had any fun money. 'No one is trying to tell you to squirrel away every cent, Roy,' Mr. White explained. 'But if you want to accomplish your goals, you must save something. I think you can see that. Luckily, there is an almost painless way to save – a way to save where you barely notice the money is gone!' "

"I might not know much about financial matters," Tom blurted out, "but I know there's no painless way to save...no way, no how."

A voice sounded from the corner of the room. "Be quiet and listen."

The source of that remark really caught me off guard. In the over twenty years I had known him, Clyde had not said one serious thing. And that's not an exaggeration. That he was even paying attention to such a no-nonsense conversation was startling, let alone that he seemed eager for it to continue.

"Clyde," Roy asked mischievously, "is there a painless way to save?"

"Sure is. *Pay yourself first.* Old Mr. White knew what he was talking about when he told you that," Clyde nodded.

"Oh, no," Tom muttered. "Don't tell me Billy Blue Jay over there is rich, too. The wealthy barber I can take, but the wealthy wacko...that's too much!"

Roy and Clyde just grinned at each other.

"Pay yourself first. I can't tell you what those three little words have meant to me," Roy reflected. "After agreeing that the ad hoc approach to saving doesn't work, and after explaining to me why the budgeting approach seldom works, Mr. White announced that the only way to save is to pay yourself first. Although he was talking about saving the ten percent, the axiom holds true for all savings. Whether you're saving for a down payment, a car, a trip, whatever, the most effective thing is to have the money come right off your pay-cheque, or right out of your bank – **before you have a chance to spend it.** But we'll talk more about saving for those kinds of items in a few months.

"Anyway, I was a bit skeptical at first. I was helping my mom and sister get by, paying my shop's rent, making car payments and trying to save for both a down payment and an engagement ring. And I wasn't meeting with much success. In my mind, there was no way I could set aside an additional ten percent. Where was I going to get that thirty dollars a month? There was nothing left at the end of the month as it was. I had tried budgeting and that hadn't worked. Then Mr. White made a very generous offer. 'Roy, you arrange to have that thirty dollars a month go directly into a separate bank account, and from there to an investment. If at any time saving that thirty dollars runs you short of funds, I'll lend you whatever you need at no interest. You can pay me back whenever it's convenient for you.'

"How could I say no? Anyway, I never did miss that money. My lifestyle didn't change at all. I know thirty dollars doesn't sound like much now, but remember it was ten percent of my income back then, and I never missed it.

"But the best example I've ever seen of the pay-yourself-first rule not adversely affecting someone's life, is Clyde.

"Good pension at work, lived in an apartment, no wife, no kids, no debt – that was Clyde fifteen years ago. Actually, that's Clyde today, too. In '73, Clyde told me he had his eye on a gorgeous twenty-thousand-dollar sailboat that he'd love to have for his retirement. You could get a heck of a boat in '73 for twenty grand. I reminded Clyde, though, that by the time he retired in '93 or so, thanks to inflation, that boat would cost a pretty penny more. The only way he would be able to afford it would be to start putting aside money right away. We started him on a couple of hundred a month...a big chunk of his income back then. 'I'll never survive,' " Roy mimicked. " 'I won't be able to go out at all. I'll have to go Dutch on my dates.'

"Clyde was convinced bankruptcy was just around the corner. Four months after we started the saving program, I asked him how he was struggling along without the two hundred dollars a month. He said, 'Geez, I'd forgotten all about that.'

"The significance of that reply can't be overstated. He'd forgotten he was even doing it! Over the years I've taught dozens of people the pay-yourself-ten-percent-first rule. Not one has noticed a dramatic change in his or her standard of living...until they're sipping martinis on their boats, that is," Roy reported, with a satisfied grin.

"Ask your dad, Dave. He'll tell you. It really is amazing. You know how quickly you adjust to your raises? Well, this is pretty much the same thing, but in reverse."

"I don't make a lot of money and I didn't start saving until fifteen years ago. But today, I'm not only looking at a boat; I'm looking at a pretty darn good retirement overall. If you three start at your age, the sky's the limit," Clyde beamed, as he gave Tom an encouraging pat on the back.

"I want to make something clear here," Roy proceeded. "At different times in your life, you're going to have to save for various things – a house, a car, a trip, whatever. A house, in particular, is a major expenditure. There is no way to achieve some goals without sacrificing your current standard of living... I mean, let's be realistic. But the ten percent saving is different. It's regular. It's a constant. You don't even see it. It comes right off your pay-cheque or out of your bank. You won't believe how easy that makes it."

"I can see that saving ten percent of your income shouldn't be too hard, especially if you pay yourself first. But I'm still curious about those fifteen percent rates of return," Tom persisted. "Last time I looked at my savings, which I admit are pitiful, they were earning a paltry six percent."

"Achieving higher rates of return over the long run is simple," Roy shrugged. "Be an owner, not a loaner."

"C'mon, Roy, I don't know anything about owning stocks or gold or real estate," Tom protested. "Hell, I saw what the market did in October '87. I want no part of that."

"Tom, you missed four key words – 'over the long run.' Ownership, at least ownership governed by common sense, will always outperform loaning in the long run. It has to. If it's consistently more profitable for businesses and individuals to leave their money in the bank than to invest it in North American enterprises, we're all in big trouble. Eventually, our whole economic system would collapse. That isn't going to happen. And in the unlikely event that it did, it wouldn't do you any good to have your money sitting down at the bank ...because the banks would all be locked," Roy laughed.

"You see, despite all the bitching and complaining and all the predictions of doom and gloom, times are good and they'll continue to get better. VCRs, microwaves, gas barbecues... your parents didn't enjoy perks like that when they were young. Technological advances, medical discoveries, social programs...do I have to go on? The fact is, we're living in great times. If you're healthy and living in Canada, you have very little to complain about, apart from the Blue Jays.

"I know we've got acid rain, deficits, unemployment problems in the East, and so on. And these are serious problems. Unfortunately, we'll always have serious problems. But the majority of them will eventually be solved. 'It is a gloomy moment in history. Not in the lifetime of any man who reads his paper has there been so much grave and deep apprehension... The United States is beset with racial, industrial and commercial chaos, drifting we know not where... Russia hangs like a storm cloud on the horizon... Of our troubles, no man can see the end.'

"Quite an editorial, don't you think? It was written in *Harper's Magazine*. Do you know when? **1847!** I think you get my point.

"I believe that the next twenty to thirty years will present some of the greatest opportunities ever. So much change. So many things happening. The only way to be a part of it all and to share in the successes is through ownership."

"So, should we buy common stocks?" I asked.

"No, with your ten percent savings, common stocks are not the way to go," was Roy's solemn warning.

Needless to say, this caught me by surprise. "You've never owned a common stock?" I questioned.

"Never. I don't know anything about stock analysis, and I don't have any friends who do, either. It's a tough game. You have to be disciplined. To perform well, you have to buy when everyone else is selling and sell when everyone else is buying, a rare combination of guts and brains. You have to have a good background in economics and you have to use that background to look into the future. You not only have to see the various companies' management teams, you have to know what questions to ask them. Most of all, you have to have a sixth sense, an intuition, a knack of recognizing value. Very few people fill the bill. I certainly don't. I mean, think about it. Do you know anybody who's become rich buying and selling stocks? There aren't many. It's just too difficult."

"What about using stockbrokers? They must know what they're doing," I asserted.

"I was a stockbroker for several years, Dave," James Murray noted, "and I can assure you that, when it comes to picking and choosing stocks, a broker is usually no better than the next guy. A comedian once said, 'A broker is someone who invests your money until you have none.' I think a more accurate line may be, 'A broker is someone who invests your money until it's his.' "

"They're around stocks all day; they must know something."

"Dave, they're salespeople. That's it. Instead of selling shoes or beds, they're selling stocks. They spend all day on the phone talking to clients, reading research reports, looking at undecipherable financial statements. In the five years I was a broker, only one guy in our office turned a profit in his personal trading account in any calendar year. One!"

"You?"

"Me? I was the worst! I thought I was a hotshot because I was driving a fancy car, eating at pricey restaurants and taking home a hefty cheque. Unfortunately, I couldn't have consistently picked winning stocks if my life had depended on it.

"After seven years, I got disgusted and quit. My commissions were great but my clients' investment performance was dismal. It hit me hard when I realized it's all a game. You know what still bothers me? Most of my clients were really happy with me. I gave excellent service, was nice on the phone, threw good cocktail parties, and knew all the right things to say. I know I could have remained a prosperous broker for years, losing people's money the whole time.

"One guy in our office was nearing retirement when I came aboard. He'd been a broker for thirty years, and was very well thought of. When he retired to his summer home and yacht, his accounts were divvied up. I got ninety of them, some very good. I started examining what he had been doing for the clients so I'd be well informed when I called to introduce myself. I'll never forget it. Of ninety accounts, only seven were up money over the years, and only one of those was up dramatically."

"Why do people stay with their brokers if they constantly lose money?" Cathy queried.

"Who knows? Some don't stay. They switch to other brokers, who often also end up losing them money. Others don't care, because they play the market for excitement more than profit. And I know this sounds hard to believe, but I'm convinced that many don't even know whether they're up or down.

"I remember one client that had been dealing with the retiring broker for fifteen years. He had started with fifty thousand and, fifteen years later, he had fifty-five thousand. 'That's better than a loss,' he said. He didn't understand that if he had just left the money in the bank, he would have had substantially more than fifty-five thousand. Like so many others, he didn't understand compound interest.

"A major reason people lose money with their brokers is that they constantly go against the wisdom of *let your profits run and cut your losses*. Most investors and brokers cut profits and let losses run.

"Good investors admit their mistakes and sell, taking small losses. Those losses are easily covered by the large profits created through a combination of buying value and exercising patience...patience that most of us don't have.

"Bad investors always think their stocks are going to come back up to at least what they cost them. Brokers know they look bad when they choose a loser so, rather than selling and accepting a loss, they perpetuate this myth. A stock doesn't know you own it – it's not going back to twenty-two so you can get out even. So, you often end up holding as the stock goes lower and lower."

"James, are you saying brokers are dishonest?" Cathy probed.

"No, no...I didn't mean it that way. I think reluctance to admit a mistake is human nature, not deliberate dishonesty. Sometimes we can't even admit to ourselves that we were wrong.

"I'd say ninety percent of the brokers I have known are professional and honest.

"The press is constantly alleging that brokers *churn* accounts, meaning they trade them excessively to generate commissions. I saw very little of that while I was a broker. For the most part, I don't think that brokers' poor investment performance has anything to do with ethics. Picking stocks successfully is very difficult, and most of us just aren't capable of doing it. It's as simple as that. And, like I said earlier, brokers are salespeople, not investment advisors. The bottom line is, if brokers were really so smart, they wouldn't need clients."

"So, we should never use a broker," Tom summarized.

"We didn't say that," Roy clarified. "We said you shouldn't invest your ten percent fund in common stocks on your own or with help from a broker. But there are a lot of fine brokers out there and, used properly, they can be a big help in achieving financial success."

"But what else does a broker do?" I questioned.

"I'll get to one of the ways a broker can help in a minute. In the meantime, let's look at how to invest that ten percent," Roy answered patiently.

"You want us to invest in ownership but not in common stocks. I guess that leaves real estate. What should we do? Buy a square foot each month with our two hundred dollars?"

Obviously, Tom was kidding, but I thought he had asked a fairly good question. Is there such a thing as a two-hundred-dollar parcel of land?

"Real estate is a very real possibility," Roy nodded. "Not by buying a square foot a month, mind you. We'll get into that later, too. First, let's look at what I think is the best alternative for investing the ten percent, at least for people under forty-five – mutual funds."

I frowned. "I thought the stock market was a losing game. Don't mutual funds own primarily common stock?"

"I've read some bad things about mutual funds lately," Cathy worried. "A lot of people lost big money in mutuals during the crash, didn't they?"

"I didn't say the stock market is a losing game. I said buying and selling stocks on your own or on your broker's advice is usually a losing game. The stock market has actually been very good to investors who have the qualities we spoke of earlier: intelligence, courage, patience and an eye for value.

"A carefully selected mutual fund gives you access to a professional money manager who demonstrates those qualities. You won't be making the individual investment decisions. A professional will.

"Simply stated, a mutual fund is a professionally managed pool of money. The pool is made up of money from people like you and me, people numbering in the thousands. We all put our money together and hand it over to someone who knows, or supposedly knows, what he or she's doing.

"There are all sorts of benefits. Most important is the one I just mentioned – professional money management. Second, mutuals give you diversification. Most people don't have enough money to buy a properly diversified portfolio, with stocks in different industries in a variety of countries. By pooling resources, individuals can gain a pro-rata share in a vast array of securities. 'Don't put all your eggs in one basket,' and all that stuff. Third, mutual funds are a *hands off* investment. There is no ongoing research and decision-making process required of the investor. This feature is very important. Most of us don't have time to look after our investments. We work all day. With mutual funds, that isn't a problem. They have a low PITA factor."

"What's a PITA factor?"

"Pain In The Ass factor...a highly technical investment term," Roy shared with a chuckle.

"You make mutual funds sound perfect. If they're so great, why do they seem to get a fair amount of bad press?" Cathy challenged.

"Oh, they're far from perfect. Like all equity vehicles, that is, investments involving ownership, they are subject to risk. There are no guarantees, and they do fluctuate up and down. If the market takes a steep fall, your mutual fund will likely tumble with it. If your professional money manager makes a series of bad investment decisions, they will be reflected in the performance of the fund, no doubt about it.

"And always bear this in mind – if you buy a common-stock fund at the height of the market, you're asking for trouble. 'Buy low, sell high' has long been a cliché of the investment business, but truer words have never been spoken. If you rush in and buy a fund, or for that matter any investment, because your neighbour's has tripled in the last five years, you're probably making a mistake. It's when your neighbour's investment has gone down thirty percent over the last two years that you're probably looking at a good time to buy.

"In addition to the fact that it's hard to time your purchase, and that mutual funds are subject to market fluctuations, there are a couple of other drawbacks.

"Mutual funds are very long-term investments. Precisely because they are hard to time and they do fluctuate, an investor has to be thinking long-term. Over a period of, say, seven to ten years, the economy, and therefore the market, will most likely continue to spiral upward. If you're willing to hold your fund for that length of time, you'll have little to worry about. But if you're buying a fund for a two- or three-year period, you better be a lot smarter than me! I'm confident that the market will perform well over the long run. It always has. But I'm not sure where it's going over the next couple of years. As I've gotten older, I've realized no one else is, either. No one. As for consistently accurate short-term forecasters, there is no such animal.

"One final problem with mutual funds – they're boring. Nobody goes to a party and talks about how their mutual fund went up two cents yesterday. Individual stocks, real estate, options, commodities, these all carry an aura of excitement...a bit of Vegas. Not funds. Nobody's ever called mutual funds an exciting way to invest your money."

"That seems like a lot of problems for what you termed our 'best alternative,' " I pointed out.

"It may seem that way, Dave, but when you examine it closely, it isn't that way at all. I'll prove it, one 'problem' at a time.

"First, market fluctuations. Like a roller coaster, they're fun on the way up, and scary on the way down. But, thanks to the power of *dollar cost averaging*, even downside fluctuations can work to your advantage.

"Dollar cost averaging is as close to infallible investing as you can get. It genuinely slants the odds in an investor's favour, yet I've read all kinds of financial planning books that haven't even mentioned it. Most people haven't even heard of it."

"I haven't," Cathy admitted. "Is it hard to do?"

"It's as easy as pie," Roy assured her. "The technical definition is, 'A system of buying common stocks or mutual fund shares at regular intervals with a fixed dollar amount.' Whoop-de-do, eh?

"Let's see how something that sounds so theoretical can easily produce fantastic results.

"Tom, say you decide to save one hundred dollars a month and invest it in fund XYZ. The month you start your program, XYZ is trading at ten dollars a share so, obviously, you buy ten shares. The second month XYZ has dropped by fifty per-cent, all the way to five dollars...not good. Your hundred dollars now buys you twenty shares. In month three, the fund has rebounded somewhat and now trades at seven dollars and fifty cents, still well under your original purchase price. You buy thirteen and a third shares. So, what's happened?"

"I've lost money following your advice. That's what happened," answered Tom.

"No, you haven't," I interrupted confidently. "You've broken even. You're down two-fifty a share on your purchase at ten, you're up two-fifty a share on your purchase at five, and you're even on your final purchase."

Roy corrected us, "You're both wrong."

"I hate math," I growled. "But how can I be wrong? It's just a question of average price. Even I can figure out the average of three numbers."

"How many shares does Tom own?" asked Roy. He then quickly answered his own question, "Forty-three and a third. And how much are the shares currently worth? Seven dollars and fifty cents each. What's forty-three and a third times seven-fifty? Three hundred and twenty-five. How much had Tom invested? Three hundred. He's up twenty-five dollars, an excellent return over such a short period of time."

"How the – "

"Because you're putting in a fixed amount each month, you obtain more shares at the lower prices. You bought twenty shares at five, but only ten at ten. Basically, it means that your average cost per share will be lower than the average price per share. In the long run, or even in the short run, that bodes well for the investor.

"So, one month when the stock market is struggling and your mutual fund is suffering accordingly, don't look at the situation and say, 'Darn, my holding is down.' Look at it and say, 'Eventually the market will go up and take the value of my holding with it, so in the meantime I'm going to pick up shares at a good price.' Dollar cost averaging is great stuff!

"With mutuals, problem number two is timing. It's very difficult for an amateur, or even a professional, to time a purchase accurately. Well, it's no problem at all when you buy monthly. We're not buying once; we're buying continually. Sometimes we'll buy high; but sometimes we'll buy low. When the market goes into a prolonged slump, there we are, picking up shares at good prices, month after month. Forget discipline, courage, intelligence and an eye for value. We don't need any of them. We buy every month.

"Does Black Monday hurt our holdings? Sure it does. But the market will bounce back. It always does. And while it's down, we're picking shares up at rock-bottom prices – a lot of shares, thanks to dollar cost averaging."

"I guess the fact that mutual funds are long-term investments isn't a problem either," Cathy mused. "We're going to be accumulating and holding shares for ten, twenty, maybe even thirty years. We are the consummate long-term investors. As you said, short-term downturns, even prolonged downturns, will work to our advantage, not to our detriment. This sounds great, Roy!"

"It is great, Cathy. And as far as mutual funds not being a glamorous investment, well, so what? After they've earned you good returns, you can use the profits to buy more exciting things if you want...such as the satellite dish I bought yesterday."

"Get out! Dave and I will be over tomorrow to watch the Tigers' game. Put a few on ice, will you, Roy?"

"I love you guys like sons, but if you ever come near my house, I'll call the police."

"Some father you must be," Tom pouted.

An intrigued Cathy pressed on. "What mutual funds should we buy, Roy, and how do we purchase them?"

"Good questions. I'm going to leave it to the three of you to select your own funds, but let me give you a few pointers.

"Too often, mutual funds are discussed in blanket terms. 'I

don't like mutual funds.' 'I heard about someone who made a killing in mutual funds.' That type of thing. But all mutual funds are not created equal. Some I like; some I don't.

"The key is the manager. You're buying professional money management and there can be as big a difference between two professional money managers as there can be between two professional hockey players. If I asked you, 'Who do you want on your team, Dave Semenko or Wayne Gretzky?' I feel certain you'd all answer the Great One. When you're selecting a fund, find the Gretzky of money management."

"How do we do that?"

"If you were assigned to select the best player in the NHL but didn't follow hockey, where would you start? You'd look at statistics, of course. Who is the highest point-getter? Who's the most consistent? Has he been good for just one year, or has he proven he can do it year after year? When times are tough and his team is struggling, does he maintain a high level of play, or drop off badly? Once you had studied the statistics, you would read some articles and talk to people in the know. What are the experts' opinions? Do they jibe with your findings?

"It's no different when you're looking for a good mutual fund. Assess past records. They don't guarantee future results, but they sure as heck are a good indication of the manager's abilities. What's the five-year average return? Ten-year? Fifteen-year? Does the fund perform consistently, or is it way up one year and way down the next? How does it fare during the bad times? Some funds have excellent records during tough times.

"Then talk to the experts. Go see a stockbroker, a mutual fund salesperson, or a life insurance salesperson. What do they think? Read a few investment publications. The *Financial Times* and the *Financial Post* do tremendous jobs monitoring mutual fund performance and highlighting industry leaders. In fact, once a month, both of these fine periodicals have in-depth mutual fund summary charts that include performance figures for various lengths of time, variability rates, commission charges, and pretty much everything else you could possibly want to know."

"Can't you give us any other tips, Roy?" Cathy pleaded. "We need all the help we can get!"

"For you, anything. Okay. Point one; make sure that if a

fund has solid rates of return, the manager who created them is still there. You're not buying past performance numbers; you're buying a manager's expertise. If fund ABC averaged twenty percent a year under the guidance of Jack Smith, but Jack Smith has left, stay away from ABC. You can't be sure what you're getting.

"Two; buy an international fund that invests across many different industries. You don't want to buy a fund that only invests in one country or one industry – that's poor diversification. Specialty funds, as they're known, are much riskier investments than international funds.

"Three; buy a fund whose manager is value-oriented. By that I mean someone who doesn't chase fads or try to be wherever the action is. Find someone who uses common sense, discipline and patience to select and hold stocks that offer good value; stocks that, at the time of purchase, others are overlooking. A broker or fund salesperson will be able to help you out here.

"Four; watch your commissions. The fund I used had a high commission structure, but it was well worth the cost. Nonetheless, it's certainly in your best interest to limit your front-end load. That load is often as high as nine percent, so that for every dollar you put in, nine cents comes right off the top. There are some good no-load funds. If you can't find one you like, remember the vast majority of load funds have fully negotiable commissions. However, the commissions should be the last factor you look at when deciding what fund to buy, and if the mutual fund salesperson you're dealing with offers good advice and solid service, a high front-end load may well be worth it.

"Five; many financial product salespeople are confined to selling only their companies' own products. This isn't necessarily bad, as many of those products are quite acceptable, but these salespeople's natural bias is something to keep in mind when weighing their advice.

"Finally, I want to re-emphasize the importance of a good long-term track record. Anybody can get hot for a few years, but if someone has had superior rates of return for a fifteen- or twenty-year period, that's a good indication that he knows what he's doing... Oops, sorry Cathy.

"As for how to buy a fund on a monthly plan, it's as easy as signing your name. All you have to do is fill out a pre-authorized chequing plan and a fund-purchase application. They're often on the same form. It won't take you more than a minute. Oh, and don't ever sign contractual plans. They limit your freedom. If the fund manager left and you wanted to switch funds, a contractual plan would restrict your flexibility through penalty clauses. Just stick to a PAC plan, a pre-authorized chequing plan, that you can cancel anytime.

"Each month,the fund will forward you a summary of your current situation: how much you contributed this month; how many shares that money bought and at what price; your accumulated share position; everything. These statements explain it all. You just stick them in your file and watch the money grow, all the while thinking what a great guy your barber is."

"Do they mail you the shares each month?"

"No. For convenience' sake, the shares are kept in non-certificate form at the mutual fund company. But if you ever want a share certificate, it's only a letter away."

"What if you want to cash out and get your money?"

"That's only a letter away, too. But you won't be doing that for a long, long time, will you, Tom?"

"Of course not, Roy. I was just curious."

I cut in, "What about taxes, Roy? Do you pay them each year?"

"That's another beauty of mutual funds compared to plain, old money in the bank. Not only do you reap the benefits of dollar cost averaging and the higher rates of return over the long run created through ownership, but you also pay a lower tax rate on your gains.

"Interest is fully taxable. Capital gains, growth that is, are not. Currently, each individual gets the first one hundred thousand dollars of capital gains tax-free and, after that, he or she pays tax on only three-quarters of the gain. And you don't pay any tax until you sell, so all your money works for you full time! Occasionally, the fund might pay a small interest dividend that is fully taxable but, with a growth fund, the type you're buying, it will be a very small amount.

"Speaking of dividends," our wealthy barber continued, "that's another thing I should explain. Mutual funds make money in three ways. Most of a growth fund's profit occurs when the fund sells stock for more than it paid for it – in other words, a capital gain. A fund also makes money when one of the stocks it owns pays it a dividend. Finally, a fund earns interest income from bonds and idle cash. At least once a year, the fund declares dividends to distribute the profits from all three of these sources. It's extremely important that, at the time of purchase, you instruct the fund management to re-invest your dividends in the form of additional shares. That's when the compounding effect really kicks in.

"One final point before we leave mutual funds. Another major reason mutual funds are preferable to just leaving your money in the bank is that they're less accessible. Very few of us have the will-power to resist the temptation that a growing bank account poses. As a result, a lot of people dip into their savings. Redeeming funds requires writing a letter, having your signature guaranteed, and registering your letter before mailing, giving us the time to think twice. These little nuisances help discourage human impulsiveness, if you will."

"You said mutual funds are probably our number one choice for investing the ten percent. What are the others?"

"Dave, my boy, there are literally hundreds of options. You could buy gold, Chinese ceramics, stamps, whatever. But for obvious reasons, those are not good choices. Certainly, mutual funds are almost perfect for our monthly savings – "

"That is, a well-selected mutual fund," I interrupted.

"That is, a well-selected mutual fund," Roy confirmed amiably. "But there is one other viable alternative. Surprisingly, it's the one Tom joked about earlier – real estate."

"How do you buy real estate for two hundred dollars a month?" Cathy and Tom chimed in stereo.

"Alas, with only two hundred a month it is impossible, but with four or five hundred, it's very possible.

"Personal loan rates, car loans for example, are running around thirteen percent right now. If you borrowed twenty thousand and amortized the loan, paid it back in full, in other words, over five years, it would cost you around four hundred and fifty dollars a month.

"But, let's say instead of using the twenty thousand to buy a car, you used it as a down payment on an eighty-thousand-dollar condominium. Your mortgage would obviously be for sixty thousand. You then rent the condo out for six hundred a month plus utilities and upkeep.

"The end result is that your rent covers your mortgage. Your expenses are covered by your tenant. Your only cost is your monthly loan payment of four hundred and fifty bucks.

"Five years later, you sell the condo for one hundred and thirty thousand dollars, a very realistic figure representing an average annual compound return of just over ten percent. Your personal loan of twenty thousand is no longer around... You've paid it off. The outstanding principal on your mortgage is around fifty-seven thousand, as most of your six-hundred-dollar monthly payment has been applied to the interest on the mortgage. One hundred and thirty minus fifty-seven is seventy-three. You are left with seventy-three thousand dollars, less your tax liability, that is. But with the one-hundred-thousand-dollar capital-gains tax exemption, most people would pay very little, if any, tax on the gain."

"Four hundred and fifty bucks a month for five years parlayed into a seventy-three-thousand-dollar profit. C'mon. It's too easy," Tom snorted.

"Not only that," James Murray added, "but there can be some tax advantages to using borrowed money to buy real estate."

"Then why isn't every man, woman and child doing it?" I asked.

"You'd be surprised how many people are doing it, or something similar to it. It's said that ninety percent of the world's millionaires have become millionaires through real estate. Mind you, it isn't as easy as it sounds. There are potential problems.

"The main one is, what happens if the property value declines instead of rising? People out in Calgary who bought in the early eighties are still trying to recover. In many cases, their proceeds from a property sale didn't even cover the mortgage balance. They had negative savings! That's a frightening concept.

"With real estate, it's a matter of timing. There's no dollar cost averaging here. No safety net. So, you'd better be right when you buy that property. The one big thing investors do have in their favour, though, is real estate's phenomenal record of rising prices. It seldom collapses. In fact, in some locales, it rarely falls at all, but...but..." Roy wagged his finger.

"The only thing worse than a bad investment is a bad investment made with borrowed money. Dave, can you see yourself telling your wife that you just lost twenty thousand dollars, twenty thousand borrowed dollars?"

"She'd kill me," I gulped, knowing the prediction was accurate.

"Kill yourself first," Tom suggested helpfully.

"The timing of the purchase isn't the only problem. Interest rates can turn against you, too. Sure, they're at twelve percent now, but what if five years down the road, when your mortgage comes due, they're back up at eighteen? Then all of a sudden your mortgage payment skyrockets to eight hundred and seventy dollars, and, because of rent control, you can't get the rent increase you need from your tenant. The heartbreak of negative cash flow results. Say this happens at a time when your business is suffering, too, Cathy. What do you do?"

"Sell."

"Sounds good, but with rates that high, very few people can afford to buy. Demand is way down, and a lot of people are trying to sell. You're not the only one hurt by the higher financing costs! End result – your property value is down. If you have no choice but to sell, you'll have to sell at a loss," he ended ominously.

"Roy, you're scaring them off the finest investment a person could make!" James Murray complained. "I mean, really, how many people do you know who have lost money in real estate?"

"I just want the kids to be aware there are risks."

"That's fine, but – "

"Hold on, hold on. Let me finish. The other problem with real estate is that it has a very high PITA factor. Finding tenants, fixing toilets at two in the morning, mowing lawns...it's a lot of work. Some people thrive on that stuff. They're great with their hands and real estate provides them with a profitable way to enjoy their hobby. But, if you're not that type of person, beware."

"The only thing I've fixed in my life is my cat," Tom kibitzed.

Jimmy and Clyde loved that one.

"So, I gather you're endorsing the fund route?" By now, my sister was on the edge of her seat.

"Initially, yes. In your early years of saving ten percent, I think the funds are a better way to go. You're busy starting your careers, raising families, buying homes, and all that. Real estate takes a lot of time. Also, the funds make more sense from a diversification standpoint, in that you'll probably own your own homes soon, so you'll already have some real estate.

"Besides, most people in their twenties, thirties, and early forties aren't in good enough financial shape to qualify for a down-payment loan, anyway – unless, of course, they borrow it privately or have a co-signer.

"What I did, and what I think you should do, is buy mutual funds with the ten percent for several years. When I had built up a good nest egg, I switched to real estate. Forgive the pun, but you don't want all your nest eggs in one basket. Plus, because I had a nest egg, I knew that if interest rates rose or real-estate prices dropped, I wouldn't be forced to sell. I had the luxury of being able to be patient. Patience is always one of the most valuable attributes in investing, and nowhere is that more true than in real estate. It may go down, but it seldom stays there.

"I've kept you three a long time today. Longer than I had planned." By the time Roy said this, Tom and I had long since had our haircuts finished. In fact, Tom needed a trim already. James Murray's grey hair was now joining our locks on the floor.

"I want to tell you a quick story before I let you go," Roy decided. "But before I do, are there any questions?"

"Should we buy more than one fund?"

"Well, Cathy, a fund, by its very nature, offers solid diversification, so I really don't think it's necessary, although it probably wouldn't hurt. Later in life, when your holding is worth a lot of money, you may want to divide it evenly among three or four funds. I never did, though."

"You talked a lot about selecting a mutual fund, but what about selecting a property?" I inquired.

"Talk to a professional. We're in the presence of greatness right here," he indicated, acknowledging James Murray. "In Kitchener, Dave, you'll have to locate someone with a good reputation. It shouldn't be hard. Ask around. In addition, there are a plethora of good real-estate books available at the library that talk about everything from selecting a good location to the tax implications of owning a property. No questions, Tom?"

"Just one. What's a 'plethora'?"

"I have another question," I stated above the laughter. "What about RRSPs and paying down the mortgage? Aren't those supposed to be smart things to do? Wouldn't they be wise investments for the ten percent?"

"Those are excellent investments, and we'll talk about both of them in the upcoming months. But the ten percent saving is different. It's separate. It's our *I've-made-it-big* fund, and it's intended to give us the finer things in life. The things we dream of one day owning and couldn't afford otherwise – a Mercedes, a winter home, early retirement...in Tom's case, a girlfriend.

"And the beauty of it is, it's not hard to do. The so-called sacrifice is barely noticeable. By saving ten percent of your pay now, you virtually guarantee yourself financial freedom later in life. Only a fool would say no to that. So, start now, and don't stop!"

"In the words of Syrus, 'Many receive advice; only the wise profit from it,' " James Murray elaborated. "Just thinking about saving ten percent has never made anyone wealthy."

"Like I said, I have just the story to convince you before you go," Roy remembered. "It will be of particular interest to you, Dave, because the individual involved is a teacher, too.

"Three or four years ago, a fellow came in. He explained that he wasn't here simply for a haircut, but also because he had heard that I'm a financial planning expert. He was wondering if he could send his twenty-two-year-old son to me to learn the basics. 'I don't know a thing about insurance, stocks, real estate...any of that stuff,' he confessed. 'The only thing I know about financial planning is to save ten percent of all you make and invest it for long-term growth. The rest of it's Greek to me.'

"Well, it turns out this man's father had been a friend of Old Mr. White's and he, too, had been fortunate enough to have learned the golden secret. He passed it along to his young son but, unlike me, this teacher hadn't furthered his knowledge of financial planning. As he said, he knew nothing about insurance and investing. What's worse, I learned through our conversation that he had abused credit cards over the years, not started an RRSP, and had lost all fifteen thousand dollars of an inheritance playing the commodities market."

"This is a real upbeat story, Roy. Very encouraging," Tom drawled, tongue in cheek.

"At the time of our meeting, that teacher's net worth was almost six hundred and fifty thousand dollars, Tom. Some of it, maybe one hundred and fifty thousand, represented his home and personal belongings. The rest of it had been created from his ten percent fund. What's more, his wife had only chosen to work for four years."

"He did everything else wrong but – " Cathy started.

"Because he had saved ten percent of each pay-cheque and

invested it for long-term growth, today he's in great shape," Roy finished.

He then walked purposefully over to the counter. A second later, we heard two clicks.Roy then turned and handed my sister a cassette tape of our entire conversation.

"I thought this might come in handy for those who don't take shorthand," he commiserated, looking pointedly at me.

"Good," I laughed. "It will save Cathy having to transcribe her notes for us. Well, Roy, what does next month's *adventure in accumulating* hold in store for us?"

"For now, why don't you three just worry about implementing this month's suggestions?" Roy responded.

"It's inspiring to know how wealthy Roy is," Tom cracked within earshot of Roy as we walked back out into the downpour. "But don't you think we're insulting him by offering to pay for our haircuts?"

"You boys," came Roy's rejoinder, "are all wet."

5
WILLS, LIFE INSURANCE AND RESPONSIBILITY

"Well, well," Roy greeted us as we came in from the sunshine. "Has it been a month already? It seems as though you three were here just last week."

"They say time flies at your age, Roy," laughed Tom.

"Cathy, you look gorgeous, as always. Tom, you don't. Hey, Dave, when's school out? Your vacation must start soon."

"Week after next. Sue and I will stick around Kitchener until mid-July, and then we'll be here for five fun-filled weeks at the cottage we've rented in Bright's Grove. You should drop by for a barbecue one night, Roy...but don't tell Clyde," I added loudly enough for Clyde to hear. He just smirked and doffed his Blue Jay baseball cap.

"Roy, you're going to be really proud of us," Cathy began, always one to turn a conversation serious. "All three of us have started our save-ten-percent programs."

"That's great! Did you use pre-authorized chequing to buy mutual funds?" Roy asked.

"Cathy and I did," I answered. "Tom went another route. But before he tells you about it, I've got a quick story for you. I was passing on what you taught us to some teachers in the staff room. They couldn't believe those compound interest examples. Even the math teachers were amazed! I explained why a monthly purchase plan of mutual funds was such a good idea...dollar cost averaging, forced saving, long-term growth... even the low PITA factor. Everything. Most of the teachers seemed really interested, but a couple were skeptical. Then Mary McGrath, our English department head, spoke up. She said that, fifteen years ago, she had started a pre-authorized chequing plan to purchase a well-known growth fund, with one hundred dollars a month. She has had all her dividends re-invested and has never withdrawn a cent. Today, her fund is worth almost eighty-five thousand dollars...and that's with only one hundred a month over a mere fifteen years! I'll tell you, that impressed them! When one of the teachers in his mid-forties asked if it was too late for him, Mary replied, 'The best time to plant an oak tree was twenty years ago. The second best time is now.' Great line, huh?"

"I couldn't have said it better myself," Roy nodded approvingly. "Obviously, starting young will benefit you tremendously, but so will starting today. Oh sure, you won't save as much starting later, but even a forty-five-year-old can still save a significant sum – very significant. As you pointed out, look what your teacher friend has accomplished in only fifteen years with a fairly small monthly saving."

"I was in my mid-forties when I started paying myself first, and I've done real good," Clyde contributed.

"I've done really well," I corrected him.

"You too, Dave? That's great," was his quick comeback.

"So, Tom, what's this other route?" Roy inquired slowly, probably still stunned by Clyde's unusual display of wit.

"Well, Roy, I know that you recommend mutual funds over real estate in the early years, but I had an opportunity I couldn't turn down.

"I told my brother what you taught us last month and he was really pumped up. He suggested that he and I go together to buy a property. The place beside his had been for sale for a couple of months. It's small and needs a lot of work, but it has definite possibilities. Brian said that if we bought it together, he would do all the yard work, and all the repairs and renovations. My job would be to find a reliable tenant and handle the paper work. We had James come out and take a look, and he agreed that, with the proximity to the water, the size of the lot, and the good neighbourhood, the property was definitely underpriced. The deal closes next month.

"We're borrowing twenty-four thousand dollars and amortizing the loan over five years. That's going to cost us two hundred and seventy dollars a month, each. We're putting twenty thousand dollars down and using the other four thousand to fix the place up a bit. Our mortgage is for fifty-seven thousand. Principal, interest and taxes are going to cost us around six hundred and seventy dollars a month."

"Have you found a tenant?" Roy asked.

"That's the beautiful part, Roy," Tom answered eagerly. "Kyle MacKenzie and his wife have signed a three-year lease with us for six hundred and eighty a month, plus utilities."

"It really is a sweet deal, Roy," James Murray broke in. "In five years I wouldn't be surprised if the place was worth a hundred and forty thousand. They've got a good tenant, balanced cash flow, low interest-rate exposure, and Tom All-Thumbs here doesn't even have to get his hands dirty."

"I'm impressed, Tom. 'You done good,' as Clyde would say. I still think that, for most young people, mutual funds are the best alternative, but you're a good example of why the word *always* is a dangerous one."

"Thanks, Roy. It's funny, but on the way here, all three of us agreed that, even though it's only been one month, we feel a lot better about our finances already. For the first time in my life, I actually believe I will be wealthy someday. It's great."

"Yeah, Roy, and you know what else?" Cathy beamed. "Like Tom said, it's only been a month, but I haven't missed that ten percent at all, just like you promised."

"Don't get a big head, Roy. Your advice last month may have been great, but I'm not all that happy with my haircut," I kidded.

"I guess I'll have to get a new bowl," Roy quipped. "Are you three ready for the second lesson? I'd better warn you, it's not quite as exciting – "

"Or as long, I hope," Tom interjected.

"Or as long," Roy confirmed. "But, in a different way, today is just as important. We're going to look at estate planning. You know...wills, life insurance...those fun things."

"And to think that I looked forward to this for a month," Cathy groaned.

"Maybe wills and insurance aren't the most thrilling topics in the world, but they sure are important. And what's more, more people foul up in this area than any other part of financial planning.

"More than half the people I know don't even have a will. That's ridiculous. And as for life insurance...well, most Canadians have the wrong kind, the wrong amount, and often even have the wrong person insured."

"Yeah. I read an article the other day saying that Canadians are overinsured," I pointed out, thinking that for once I'd look informed.

"Wrong," replied Roy. "Dead wrong. Being the most insured country on a per capita basis and being overinsured are not synonymous. Canadians, for the most part, are not overinsured. Some obviously are, but the majority of us are underinsured... in some cases, dramatically...even alarmingly so.

"But we'll talk more about insurance in a few minutes. First I want to deal with wills.

"You know estate planning is really nothing more than what you do before you die to make sure that the people and things that you care about are well taken care of after your death. You want your *living estate*, in other words, your assets less your liabilities, combined with your insurance proceeds, to provide the necessary capital to carry out your wishes. Your will should make sure that that capital is distributed according to your wishes.

"The importance of an up-to-date will cannot be overstated. Contrary to what most people believe, if you die without a will, things will not automatically work out as you would have wished. Disaster can result.

"Dave, let's say your father were to die tomorrow. If he didn't have a will, what do you think would happen?"

"My mother would inherit everything?" I hazarded, shrugging my shoulders.

"No. I bet the court decides. They'll look at how many children there are, how old they are, and all that stuff," Cathy ventured, in a somewhat more confident tone.

"You're both wrong," stated Roy. "When no will is available, the estate assets are frozen and the court winds up the deceased's affairs and pays off his or her debts. The remaining estate is then divided according to a rigid set of rules found in the provincial intestacy laws."

"Intestacy?" Cathy and Tom echoed in chorus.

"Intestacy, from intestate...having made no will," Roy explained.

"No thought is given to the deceased's known wishes or to the needs of the potential inheritors. For example, even if a surviving spouse needed a great deal of money for medical reasons, the estate would still be allotted according to the rules. The bulk of the estate might be tied up in a government-administered trust until the children reached the age of majority.

"If your father died, the first seventy-five thousand dollars would go to your mother. The remainder of the estate would be divided, one-third for your mother, two-thirds for you two kids."

"So, in our case, the remainder would be one-third each," I summarized.

"Exactly, although the Family Law Act may come into play.

"Regardless, I think you'll agree with me that it's your dad's wish for your mom to have everything and then, upon her death, for you children to inherit the family estate. Who knows? Over the years she may need the entire amount."

"Boy, you two had better hope your dad doesn't have a will," cracked Jimmy.

"Charitable donations, scholarship awards, gifts for grand-children or godchildren...none of these will be taken care of if there is no will.

"Even if you're single, you should have a will. Cathy, if you died tomorrow, your entire estate would go to your parents. That may be what you want but, more than likely, it isn't," Roy continued.

"You're right, Roy, it isn't. I'd like to leave Dave and Sue something. I mean, they need it more than Mom and Dad do. And I'd like to leave the Big Sister organization something for all the fine work they do. And, Dave and Sue have asked me to be godmother to their baby. I never thought about it before, but I really do need a will."

"Me, too," I added. "When I die, I want to make sure every-thing goes to Sue and doesn't get tied up in a trust for years. That's no good."

"Even I need a will," mused Tom. "I'm not really all that close to my dad, and even if I was, he certainly doesn't need the money as much as my brother and sister do."

"Don't forget your best friend, either," I reminded him.

"All right. I don't think it's necessary to go around the room stating why each of us needs a will, or you'll end up being here longer than you were last month. The point is that everyone does need a will, period. We haven't even talked about prob-lems that intestacy can cause for common-law spouses and business partners. It gets pretty scary."

"How do you make a will?" wondered Cathy.

"First, don't do it yourself. Go to a professional. Most lawyers have experience in drawing up wills and in estate planning.

"Second, before you go to a lawyer, sit down and map out

exactly what your estate would consist of and how you want it to be divided. If you're married, make sure your spouse sits down with you.

"Third, choose an executor. This is the person or trust company that will carry out your will's instructions. The executor has to do everything from making the funeral arrangements, to notifying the beneficiaries, to applying for Canada Pension Plan benefits, to filing an income tax return, and a lot more. It is a heavy responsibility.

"So, if you choose an individual as an executor, make sure he or she lives near you. It's unfair to ask your cousin Eddy to fly across the country to wind up your affairs, especially since it may involve several trips. Also, choose someone your age or younger. It doesn't make sense to name your father or aunt as executor, when the odds are they'll predecease you. And don't be too quick to name your spouse! If he or she has no money management skills, there may be other, more suitable choices. Besides, your spouse is going to have a hard enough time without having to handle all the work involved in being an executor. Co-executors are a good alternative. Your spouse and a friend with a business background would be perfect. Two final points about choosing an executor: One; for obvious reasons, choose someone who is absolutely honest and reliable. Two; don't forget to name contingent executors in case your first choice is unwilling or unable to act when the time comes."

"Boy, you sure were right, Roy," Tom commented.

"About the importance of a will?"

"No. About this not being as exciting as last month."

"Ha, ha! Actually, you'll find the part on insurance very interesting. Just let me wrap up wills.

"A fourth thing to keep in mind is that large potential capital-gains taxes, business ownership, divorces, alimony, remarriages, et cetera, et cetera, all can complicate the estate-planning process. Make sure the lawyer you're using is fully aware of any potential problem areas. Lawyers know how to plan for all the standard problems, like the simultaneous death of two spouses, but they're not mind-readers. They can't know all the relevant details of your personal situation unless you tell them.

"The fifth and final point to keep in mind is that you must keep your will updated. Births, deaths, divorces, business deals, whatever, may make a will obsolete. Review your will at least once a year and, for heaven's sake, make sure that your executors know where to find it! In fact, give them a copy and keep another copy at your lawyer's.

"Oh, and always keep a complete, up-to-date net-worth statement, listing everything you own and everything you owe, along with a copy of your will, in your safety deposit box. A friend of mine died ten years ago and they didn't discover until last year that he owned shares in a number of large companies. The certificates were registered in the brokerage company's name and held on account, and the firm had never been notified of his death. A lawyer that I know tells me this kind of thing happens frequently."

"How much does it cost to draw up a will?" I inquired.

"A straightforward will, the kind most of us need, costs around one hundred dollars. In view of its importance, that's certainly not a lot of money to spend."

"I don't know why, but I always figured a will would cost a lot more than that."

"No. It's not the cost of a will that prevents most Canadians from having one. It's just pure procrastination. We all know we're going to die someday, but we don't want to admit that day could be soon, so we put off planning for it. But you three won't do that. Do you know how I can be so sure?"

"Because you know we're responsible people?" Tom speculated.

"No. Because next month each of you is going to bring me a copy of your lawyer's bill showing that you've had a will drawn up. If you don't, the fountain of your financial knowledge will suddenly dry up."

"Roy," Cathy protested, "we're not little kids. We're mature adults."

"Speak for yourself!" Tom roared.

"We all started our save-ten-percent program without being forced to, didn't we?" my sister persevered.

"Good point, Cathy. Very good point. But bring me the bill anyway," Roy commanded, over the chuckles of James Murray.

Procrastination is my middle name, but I didn't need Roy's strong-arm tactics to get me moving. After learning about intestacy laws, I decided that only a fool wouldn't have a will. One hundred dollars is an insignificant price to pay when you consider what's at stake.

"The bottom line is, Roy, that if you don't have a will, your loved ones could suffer," I concluded aloud. "I'm not going to do that to my survivors."

"Well said, Dave. But bring me the bill next month anyway."

"Roy did the same thing with me," Clyde piped up. "Treated me just like a kid. You know what I did to get him back? I bequeathed him my little dog."

"I can't believe that," James Murray scoffed.

"It's true. You can ask Roy."

"No, no. Not the part about the dog. What I can't believe is you knowing the word 'bequeath'!"

"Just be sure Mrs. Murray wears a name-tag to my funeral, James," Clyde warned him. "I worry that Roy might accidentally take her home with him, and leave my dog alone back in my apartment."

"I hate to break up this scintillating dialogue, but we've got more material to cover." Roy's announcement immediately silenced Sarnia's Laurel and Hardy.

"On to insurance. Let me caution you now to pay strict attention to the rest of today's lesson. I say this for four reasons: One; the financial future of your loved ones may depend on you having the proper amount of life insurance. Two; it is, without a doubt, essential to your own financial future that you have the right type of life insurance. Three; there is a good chance that James and I are the only two people you'll ever meet who have a full understanding of insurance, and who are willing to share that understanding with you. And four; my tape recorder is broken."

"What about insurance agents?" Cathy asked.

"Are you kid – "

"Whoa, slow down, James. Slow down," interrupted Roy. "We'll talk more about insurance agents in a few minutes. For now, suffice it to say that there are some good insurance agents and some who are not so good."

"Many who are not so good," James Murray grumbled.

"Perhaps," Roy agreed. "But that holds true in any occupation. There are good teachers and bad teachers, good real-estate agents and bad real-estate agents – "

"Good-looking wives and bad-looking wives," Clyde shot at James.

"The problem with insurance is that most people are so

poorly informed that they have no way of telling the good agent from the bad agent. If I consistently give you a bad haircut, you'll eventually stop coming here."

"Gee, we haven't yet," I remarked.

"Cute, Dave. But with an insurance agent's advice, it's different. It's intangible. Its worth can only be measured by an informed observer. So, the answer is simple – become an informed observer! Fortunately, that's not as difficult as you might think.

"Let's get started. Cathy, why do people buy life insurance?" Roy asked.

"Well, uh, what do you mean?" she stammered, surprised to be singled out.

"Just what I said. Why do people buy life insurance?"

"Well, if you die prematurely, you want to have enough money to support your spouse and kids, I guess."

"Close. People buy, strike that, **should** buy life insurance so that when they die, their living estate, again, that is their assets less their liabilities, combined with their insurance proceeds, can allow for the proper winding down of their financial affairs, and provide the desired standard of living for their dependents. Now, that's pretty basic, isn't it?"

A collective "yes" was offered.

"Fine," Roy nodded as he turned back toward Cathy. "Bearing that in mind, how much insurance do you need, Cathy?"

"I just bought a fifty-thousand-dollar policy."

"I didn't ask how much you have. I asked how much you need," Roy reminded her politely.

"Apparently not fifty thousand dollars," Cathy frowned. "I don't know... I guess..." She paused to think.

"How much would your dependents need?" Roy helped.

"I don't have any dependents," my puzzled sister responded.

Roy nodded his head slowly and emphatically.

"None. You're saying I don't need any life insurance?"

"That's precisely what I'm saying. Life insurance is a wonderful thing. It is, no doubt, the most important of all financial products. It is a must until a sufficient living estate has been acquired to protect one's dependents. Purchased properly, it provides people with a relatively inexpensive way to guarantee their dependents a targeted standard of living if premature death occurs. Really, life insurance is better termed *financial protection for dependents*, or *income replacement in-*

surance. But despite all that, you have to remember it is still an expense. The life insurance companies aren't giving it away. So, like everything else that costs money, you only want to buy it when you have a need for it.

"Think about car insurance for a moment. It's a wonderful product, too. But no one in his right mind would buy it if he didn't own a car. Well, buying life insurance when you have no need for it is equally foolish."

"Shouldn't I at least have enough insurance to cover my funeral expenses?" Cathy wondered.

"In addition to taking care of your dependents, your living estate and your insurance proceeds combined must also allow for the proper winding down of your financial affairs. That includes eliminating all debts, settling taxes, treating business partners and employees fairly, and paying funeral expenses. If your living estate is sufficient to do that, no insurance is needed. For most single people, that's the case," Roy replied.

"Hmm..." Cathy started slowly. "My assets would definitely cover my debts and my funeral costs, with money left over."

"Mine, too," Tom realized. "As of right now, I don't have any debts and the twenty-five-thousand-dollar group insurance coverage I get as a benefit at work should cover my funeral."

"Twenty-five thousand! That's a heck of a funeral," Clyde whistled. "I'll look forward to it, Tom."

"Theoretically, this sounds fine, Roy, but I have a few questions," Cathy persisted. "When I bought my policy last week, the agent insisted it was the smart thing to do for a number of reasons. Some of those reasons still seem to make sense, even though I have no dependents. The first is that my policy is also acting as a saving vehicle for my retirement. The second is that insurance is cheaper to buy when you're young. The third is that I should buy insurance now, when I know I can get it. I can't be sure that in five years, when I may need it, I'll still qualify for it."

"Nonsense, nonsense and nonsense," muttered James Murray, still glaring at Clyde over his coffee.

"Quite frankly, James is right," Roy conceded. "None of those reasons holds water. You'll see that as we continue our lesson. In fact, if you pay close attention, you'll be able to explain yourself why each of those reasons for buying is 'nonsense.'

"Right now, though, I want to concentrate on how to analyze

your insurance needs properly. Tom, how much insurance do I need?"

"Zero. Your living estate, as you put it, is sufficient to provide for your wife and kids. You are, after all, the wealthy barber," Tom answered confidently.

"By George, I think he's got it!" Roy turned to me. "Dave, how much insurance should you buy on your baby's life?"

"Zero. No one is dependent on the baby," I replied, with equal confidence.

"Very good," our instructor said approvingly. "Although we love them dearly, children are financial liabilities, not assets. You don't insure a liability! If you had an uncle move in with you, eat your food, drink your beer and watch TV all day, would you insure him? Of course not! He's a liability. Although parents would cringe at that comparison, I hope you three get the point.

"You only buy insurance when there is a definite need to protect your dependents and to help in winding down your financial affairs. Single people, therefore, often don't need insurance. Young married couples, especially those with children, almost always need insurance. The question for them then becomes not, 'Do we need it?' but, 'How much do we need?'

"Often the answer to that is, 'More than you think.' Your living estate, not including your non-investment assets, plus your insurance proceeds must provide enough capital to accomplish a number of things. One; all debt **must** be paid off. The last thing the surviving spouse needs is to be saddled with debt. Two; enough capital must be available to cover future lump-sum obligations. This is something that is often forgotten...your funeral expenses, for example. A better example, though, would be college expenses for the children. It costs quite a bit of money to send a child to college or university. Although the child should be responsible for a fair amount of the total cost, he or she may need help. That money to help has to come from somewhere. It should be taken into account when analyzing insurance needs. Three; there must be enough capital and other sources of income present to provide sufficient cash flow to support your dependents. If you feel that your family would need forty thousand dollars a year to live comfortably and their non-investment income after your death would be only ten thousand, your living estate and insurance

proceeds would then have to provide a block of capital sufficient to bring in the other thirty thousand dollars annually.
How much is that? Well, unfortunately, most people arrive at
that answer by assuming they will always be able to earn a
guaranteed ten percent on their money. That assumption
leads them to believe they need a capital pool of three hundred
thousand dollars."

"I don't see any problems with that logic," I confessed.

"The problem is that you can't be sure you'll always be able
to earn a ten percent rate of return. When it comes to loved
ones, you're better to err on the conservative side. I would base
my calculations on an eight percent assumed rate of return.
So, to generate thirty thousand dollars, I would need a three-
hundred-and-seventy-five-thousand-dollar pool of capital.

"The last thing your living estate plus insurance proceeds
must cover is often totally neglected by people. **Inflation!** Inflation is a widow's or widower's number one enemy. For example, an insurance program is designed so that a widow is
left with an annual income of thirty-five thousand dollars, the
desired amount. The problem is that the entire thirty-five
thousand is needed to support the family; none is saved for
the future. Ten years later, that thirty-five thousand may be
worth only fifteen thousand in purchasing-power terms. A
middle-aged, untrained woman is forced to go back to work
and, even then, the family has trouble surviving. Unlikely?
Hardly! That's exactly what happened to my wife's aunt...and
to many, many other people. Inflation's eroding effect on purchasing power is as powerful as compound interest's growth
effect on monthly savings. It must be taken into account. It
sometimes means buying up to an additional one hundred
thousand dollars of coverage. But so be it. It must be done.

"Dave, let's look at your case. Pretend that it's a year from
now. You've bought your home, and you and Sue are proud
parents. How much insurance do you need? And how much
insurance should you buy on Sue's life?"

"With our down-payment fund gone toward the purchase of
the house, we won't have any investment assets to speak of,
so the insurance proceeds are going to have to cover all of Sue's
and the baby's needs," I started.

"Good," Roy commended me. "Continue."

"First, we'll have to have a lump sum available to eliminate
our debts. I should say debt. The only money that we'll owe

will be our mortgage of, say, eighty thousand.

"Future lump-sum obligations. Hmm... Davey Junior's college education, the funeral expenses, and within a couple of years, a new car."

"Fifteen thousand should more than cover the education costs. There will be eighteen years to invest the money and make it grow," Roy explained.

"And ten thousand for burial costs and fifteen thousand for the car. So, future lump-sum obligations total forty thousand," I tallied. "Then there's the need for a sufficient income. You know, I don't want Sue to feel she has to work outside the home...especially before the baby's in school. So, I think I'm going to assume her income after my death will be confined to the ten thousand dollars a year she makes freelancing as a travel writer. To live comfortably, she'll probably need around thirty thousand a year. With no debt and no rent to pay, that should be plenty."

"You know what I would do, Dave?" Cathy suggested. "If she could live comfortably on thirty thousand dollars, I would buy enough insurance to give her an income of thirty-three thousand. You know why? So she could continue the save-ten-percent program without cramping her lifestyle."

"You know, you kids aren't nearly as slow as your father says you are," Roy joshed. "That's great thinking, Cathy. Dave, I'm sure you'd agree that Sue deserves not only to live comfortably, but also to have the finer things in life. Well, you've learned how she can!"

"Thirty-three thousand it is," I concurred. "To create an investment income of twenty-three thousand a year, assuming an eight percent interest rate, I would need how much, Roy?"

"Two hundred and eighty-seven thousand dollars...give or take a few hundred," James Murray intervened, proudly showing Clyde the calculator on his watch.

"As for inflation," I went on, "I really don't think I'd need that much. With Sue saving ten percent and with her likely, in fact certain, to re-enter the travel agency business when the baby gets a little older, she should be fine." I looked around smugly.

"Excellent, Dave," Roy congratulated me. "The last bit on inflation was very well thought out. That's the type of analysis we all have to do on our insurance needs. It is imperative that we not buy too little insurance, but it is also important that we not buy too much. Did you total how much insurance you decided you needed? Four hundred and seven thousand dollars worth."

I was dumbfounded.

"He won't be able to afford his premiums, will he?" asked Tom, who, uncharacteristically, seemed genuinely concerned.

"I get twenty-five thousand dollars coverage free with my benefit package, but I'll still have to buy almost four hundred thousand worth. I'll need the insurance," I griped. "Paying the premiums is going to kill me!"

"Dave, my boy, you're wrong. If you buy the proper types of insurance, your premiums will be quite reasonable. For now, though, let's stick to the amounts and not get ahead of ourselves.

"Making the same assumptions...house, baby, et cetera... how much insurance should you place on Sue's life?" Roy then asked.

"Sue's no longer working at the travel agency, so our current family income would only drop by the ten thousand dollars she makes selling her travel articles. But the expenses would also drop with one less person to support. With my income being fairly good, I'm going to say zero. No insurance on Sue's life."

"I can see your logic, Dave – " Roy conceded.

"But..." I anticipated.

"But I want to make two points. Always insure both spouses for at least the amount of the outstanding debt, in your case, eighty thousand dollars. A debt-free balance sheet substantially reduces stress, along with freeing up cash flow. Raising a child, making payments on an eighty-thousand-dollar mortgage and enjoying a good standard of living wouldn't be easy on your salary alone. Also, you've forgotten a couple of expenses that would result from Sue's death. One; funeral costs of ten thousand dollars. Two; day-care for your young child. With no debt, I'll agree that you won't need to replace the entire income from Sue's writing, but you want at least enough to cover the cost of child-care."

"So, I probably need two hundred thousand dollars coverage on Sue," I surmised. "Eighty thousand to pay off the mortgage, ten thousand for the funeral and the rest to pay for a nanny for a few years."

"The point of all this was not just to help Dave." Roy motioned toward Tom and Cathy. "It's to help you two bored-looking individuals, as well. There may be a woman out there crazy enough to want Tom as a husband. There might be an even crazier man who would tolerate Dave as a brother-in-law. So, eventually you may both be in the position of needing insurance. And when you are, you've got to be able to figure out exactly how much you need. All it takes is the knowledge I've given you – remembering the four needs for insurance proceeds – and some common sense."

"I'm going to talk to my brother about this tomorrow, Roy." Tom shook his head disbelievingly. "He's got two young children and a wife. I now know for a fact that he doesn't have nearly enough insurance. He has one hundred and fifty thousand dollars coverage through work, but that's it."

"You may be doing him the biggest favour of his life...or at least doing his loved ones the biggest favour of **his** life," replied Roy. "Now, before we move on to the different types of insurance, let me give you three illustrations of some tricky evaluations you may be faced with in the future.

"One; both spouses are working and making excellent money. That situation could arise, for example, if Cathy married a doctor. They analyze their insurance needs and decide that if either of them died, the other could carry on quite comfortably, at least financially, on his or her own without insurance proceeds. Their house is fully paid for, and their two children could easily be supported on either parent's income. What's wrong with their analysis?"

For a few seconds, everyone was silent. Then I realized where Roy was headed. "What if they both die at the same time? Their children would be left with only the house."

"Excellent, Dave! Does everyone see? James, didn't you tell me about a case just like that?" Roy prodded.

"Yes. That happened to friends of Barb's parents several years ago. You have to protect against situations like that by buying a policy that pays only when both of the insureds die," answered James.

"All right. A second example," Roy continued without missing a beat as Tom got into the barber chair, "Cathy sells half of her business to Joe Schmoe. A year later, Joe dies, leaving his half to his wife, who has no business experience. She has no desire to enter the business world and decides that she wants to sell her half back to Cathy. Unfortunately, Cathy has no liquid reserves and has exhausted her lines of credit. Suddenly her life line, Richardson Landscaping, is in jeopardy. Will it be shut down? Will Schmoe's half be sold to an inappropriate person?"

"I should have had insurance on **his** life. Is that what you're saying?" asked Cathy.

"Yes. It's another example of how difficult it can be to analyze how much insurance to buy. It's not enough that you are properly insured so that your loved ones will be taken care of. You also have to make sure that anyone you're dependent upon is properly insured."

Since I'm not dependent on anyone, this point didn't strike me as too important. It sure had an impact on Tom, though.

"Hey!" he blurted out, stopping Roy in mid-snip. "Lucky you gave that example! If my brother were to die after we close our real-estate deal, I'd be in trouble. I couldn't afford to pick up the payments on his half of the down-payment loan. I'm going to have to talk to him about us getting insurance on each other's lives."

"Take care of that soon," Roy encouraged him. "One final example of insurance-needs analysis. Fifteen years from now, Tom has parlayed his monthly savings and apparent knack for buying undervalued properties into a seven-hundred-thousand-dollar real-estate empire. Unfortunately, he is hit by a bus." This drew applause from both Jimmy and Clyde. "Included in the seven-hundred-thousand-dollar valuation is three hundred thousand dollars worth of capital gains, which translates into a tax liability of approximately one hundred thousand dollars. Tom felt he was self-insured, so the estate was limited to his personal residence, real-estate holdings and baseball-card collection. So, his wife who, incidentally, was driving the bus" – this remark caused me to cough my Pepsi out onto my white golf shorts – "is forced to sell a property to pay the tax bill. Sadly, real estate is at its lowest point in two decades, making it a terrible time to sell. But she has no choice. The point is that, for liquidity reasons, it would have been a good idea for Tom to carry enough insurance to cover his tax liability.

"I gave these three examples to show you that a lot of thought is needed to correctly analyze your insurance needs. Don't be lazy. Do the necessary thinking. Get a book out of the library. Talk to an insurance agent. They've had years of experience and have encountered almost every possible scenario. For heaven's sake, be insured for the correct amount! You owe it to yourself and to your family."

Tom's haircut was coming along nicely, and it was now obvious to everyone that Roy's promise of this month's lesson being shorter than last month's had a better-than-even chance of being broken. We hadn't even delved into the different types of insurance policies. I had nightmarish visions of Tom and me missing our tee-off time.

"Roy, I don't mean to sound unappreciative because I'm far from it. I can't believe how much we've learned again today, but Tom and I are supposed to meet Dad at Huron Oaks in less than an hour. With all the different types of policies still to be discussed, could we perhaps finish this off next month?"

"That won't be necessary, Dave. Although, as you pointed out, there are a number of different types of policies, there is only one that you, Cathy and Tom will probably ever need – *renewable and convertible term insurance.* It won't take me long to teach you why.

"I'm sure that even you three, with your limited financial backgrounds, have heard of the age-old argument of whole life versus term, better stated as cash-value insurance versus term insurance."

"I certainly have," remarked Cathy. "You won't believe this, but when I went to buy insurance last month, I actually decided to do a little research beforehand. All three books I read suggested that term insurance was a better alternative than cash-value insurance. Yet both agents I saw were very insistent that I buy cash-value. I bowed to their expertise and bought a *universal life* policy."

"I don't even know the difference," Tom admitted candidly.

James Murray leapt in, "Those agents recommended cash-value because – "

"Hold on, James," Roy ordered. "You'll have your chance. First, let's look at a couple of definitions.

"Term insurance is like fire insurance. It pays out the face amount of the policy if the insured dies, just as fire insurance pays out the face amount if the insured building burns down. Term insurance is in force for a stipulated length of time – or term – hence its name. It's most often sold in one-year, five-year, ten-year or twenty-year terms. When the term expires, so does the insurance. There are no cash values, savings, or investment elements. It is insurance in its most basic and least expensive form.

"Cash-value insurance is basically a combination of term insurance and a forced-savings program, with the savings program being the cash-surrender value of the policy. Dave, are the odds of you dying next year if you own a cash-value insurance policy higher or lower than the odds of you dying next year if you own a term policy?"

"The same, of course. Even I know that."

"Yes, I think anyone could answer that question correctly. It's the significance of the answer that most people miss," Roy explained patiently.

Damn. He had lost me. "I'm not sure I follow you."

"I'm sure you've heard the expression, 'Buy term and invest the difference.' What does it mean to you?" Roy put the ball back in my court.

"Well, instead of buying a cash-value policy, you buy the same amount of term coverage, which is less expensive because it doesn't include a savings element. Then you invest the difference between the two costs in a savings vehicle."

"That's right. So, remembering your answer to the *odds of dying* question, what's wrong with the oft-heard question, 'Am I better to buy term and invest the difference or to buy a cash-value policy?' I'll tell you what's wrong. They are the same thing. As you said, the odds of dying are the same, regardless of what type of policy you buy. So, there is really only one type of life insurance, and that is pure protection based on a mortality table. That's what term insurance is. Cash-value insurance is pure protection, or term insurance, plus a cash-value element. 'Buy term and invest the difference' is exactly what a cash-value policy does. The problem is, it doesn't invest that difference nearly as well as you can on your own."

"If that's the case, why do insurance companies issue cash-value products? And why do agents sell them?" asked Cathy.

"Because both companies and agents often put their own interests ahead of their clients'," James Murray responded hotly, before Roy had a chance to speak. "The premiums on cash-value policies are much higher – and so is the commission rate! The companies and agents make far more money by selling cash-value insurance than they could by selling term."

"You're pretty agitated, James!" Cathy exclaimed. "Do you agree with him, Roy?"

"No. With all due respect, James, I don't. Sure, there are a number of unscrupulous salespeople but, as I said earlier, I don't think it's any worse in the insurance industry than in any other business. Maybe it was fifteen years ago, when James was an agent. But now many agents do a conscientious job not only of placing insurance, but also of estate and financial planning. The products have improved, and so have their prices. Now you can get price distinctions based on sex and based on smoking versus non-smoking, for example. Professionalism is definitely on the rise, too. More and more agents are becoming better educated about all financial matters, not just insurance."

"If all that's true, why do they sell so much of what you claim is an inferior product?" Cathy persisted.

"Yes! If all that's true, why do they sell so much of what you claim is an inferior product?" James Murray echoed.

"The policy I just bought on my agent's recommendation was a cash-value policy," Cathy remarked, before Roy could offer a response.

"First, let me say that not all agents do push cash-value policies. Many have seen the light and now sell primarily renewable and convertible term insurance. Many are also espousing the benefits of paying yourself first, saving ten percent, and building a registered retirement savings plan. Those people are doing good jobs for their clients.

"Second, those who do sell cash-value insurance believe they are doing the right thing. They believe, and rightly so, that it is vital not only to have the proper amount of coverage, but also to become self-insured through saving and investing. For obvious reasons, insurance costs increase dramatically later in life. So, you have to have saved the funds necessary to pay them, or to have saved enough not to even need insurance in your later years. Most agents feel a cash-value policy accomplishes this goal of saving while, at the same time, insuring you.

"They argue that although 'Buy term and invest the difference' sounds good in theory, it seldom works in practice. Why? Because for most people the more accurate expression is 'Buy term and spend the difference.' Agents see that a lot of clients don't have the discipline or the knowledge to invest the difference. So, even though they start out properly insured with inexpensive term coverage, they end up facing a retirement that includes high insurance costs and an empty bank account."

"Do most people end up that way?" I wondered.

"Unfortunately, a lot do. It's staggering the number of people over the age of fifty-five who are in serious financial trouble. But you won't be," Roy assured us.

"How can you be so certain?"

"Because you're getting financial advice from the wealthy barber. Between your ten percent fund and your retirement planning, you'll be self-insured at a very reasonable age – very reasonable. You're not only buying term and investing the difference; you're investing more. And you're investing it well!"

"That sounds great, Roy. But if the insurance company is offering to do it all for you by selling cash-value insurance – insurance plus savings – why not let them? Won't they do a better job investing than we would, anyway?"

Cathy's question seemed justified.

"No!" was Roy's resounding answer. "Normally, the savings portions of cash-value policies are comparatively poor investments! Tom, if I came to you and said the following, would you save with me? 'To save at our institution, you must buy life insurance. You must pay for it even if you don't need it. We'll take everything you deposit in the first year for ourselves. In future years, we'll charge you to deposit money into your savings account. You can borrow the money at any time, but we'll charge you interest. If you happen to die while this loan is outstanding, we'll decrease the amount we were to pay your beneficiary by the outstanding amount of the loan. If you don't borrow from this account and you die, we'll pay the beneficiary only the face amount of the policy – we'll keep your savings for ourselves. Oh, and finally, we don't offer the greatest rates of return.' "

"No, thanks. I think I'll keep buying houses with my brother. You know, I always thought it was too good to be true that you could often borrow from your insurance policy at a low interest rate. But paying any interest to borrow your own money isn't that good a deal, is it?"

"Say, Tommy boy. If you thought being able to borrow your own money from your policy at five percent was a good deal, you'll love my offer," James Murray wheedled facetiously. "I'll lend you your money out of your bank account and only charge you four percent! Sounds good, eh?"

"You see," Roy went on, "the deal I offered Tom isn't far removed from the deal offered by the traditional cash-value policy. In a way, you can't blame insurance companies for trying to make money. They have to cover expenses, pay their agents and make a profit for their shareholders. That can't leave much for you, the policyholder. To save successfully, you have to cut out the middleman – "

"And you have to invest for growth," a fervent Tom interrupted.

"A good point indeed. As we saw last week, the last thing we want is our long-term savings tied up earning low rates of return. We want to be owners, not loaners," Roy reminded us.

"You mentioned that if we buy a traditional cash-value policy and die, all we get back is the face value of the insurance we have paid for. The insurance company keeps our savings. That seems almost illegal," I remarked.

"That's one point on which James and I are in full agreement," Roy sighed. "For years, the insurance companies virtually stole the savings of many of their policyholders. In fact, some companies still issue policies that keep the savings portion upon the death of the insured. That's not fair, and there is no defense for it. Fortunately, most agents and companies are getting away from that type of product."

"The premium you pay for those policies covers the costs of two services: protection for your dependents if you should die; and protection for yourself if you should live. You pay dearly for both those services but, unless you have mastered the impossible trick of being simultaneously alive and dead, you are restricted to receiving the benefits of only one service. It's a terrible deal!" pointed out James Murray.

"There is one other point I'd like to make here. Some agents agree that cash-value policies might not be the best way to save, but argue that they're still worthwhile because they are compulsory savings plans. That," Roy snorted, "is nonsense. If you have the self-discipline to make premium payments over a long period of time, you certainly have the self-discipline to manage a suitable savings program on your own. In fact, you three have already started."

"I'm confused by one thing." Cathy stared at Roy intently. "The cash-value policy I bought last week was a lot different than the traditional one you two are describing. It's called universal life, and my agent assures me that the rates of return

are very competitive. He also told me that, when I die, my beneficiary gets both the insurance proceeds and the policy's
savings component. In fact, I can even invest the savings in a
vehicle similar to a mutual fund if I want to. That doesn't sound
like a bad deal, does it?"

"Universal life is a great example of what I said earlier. The
insurance industry really has improved its product line over
the last few years. Universal life is a much better product than
the traditional whole life policy. It unbundles the insurance
and savings elements, meaning that when you die, as you said,
your beneficiary will receive both. It also offers more competitive rates of return. That being said, though, for a couple of
reasons it still isn't as good as buying term and investing the
difference. First, the term insurance component may be purchased much more cheaply outside the package. Second, because the company has to cover expenses and make a profit,
the investment/savings portion will not yield as great a return
inside the package as outside. This is especially true if you
cash in the policy in the early years, as the insurance company's fixed costs on each policy are very high. If, for example,
after ten years you cancel your universal life policy because
you no longer need the insurance, the rate of return on your
savings component is usually only in the three percent area –
which is ridiculous.

"Universal life does have one major benefit, and that is that,
at the moment, the savings portion is allowed to grow tax-free.
But because of the normally inferior rates of return and the
comparatively high costs of the term component, that advantage is negated. The bottom line still is – buy term and invest
the difference.

"Cash-value policies carry level premiums whereas term becomes more expensive as you get older. Why is that?" Roy
tested us.

"I know," Tom stated. "It's because, with cash-value policies, you overpay in the early years to subsidize the rising costs
in the later years. The overpayment is invested and compoun-
ded so the rising costs in later years are easily covered."

"Tom, I'm impressed." Roy's compliment was genuine. "Is
this a good thing?"

Tom spoke up again. "No. It's 'nonsense,' as James would
say. Why overpay in the early years when there's a good chance
you won't even need the coverage in the later years? I'll be self-

insured by the time my term insurance costs become expensive. Also, when you're younger you need the money more. You have more responsibilities. It's a bad time to be overpaying for insurance."

"Tom, I take back all the things I've thought about you over the years. You are definitely smarter than the average bear," remarked Roy.

"Bear, perhaps, but not human," I muttered, belying the fact that I was impressed.

"Okay. I see that term insurance is the way to go, but what about my agent's argument that buying insurance now was a good idea so I would guarantee future insurability?" Cathy absent-mindedly pushed a fallen lock of hair with her toe. "That seems to make sense, doesn't it? Why did James label that as 'nonsense' ?"

"I'll answer that, Roy," James Murray offered. " 'Nonsense' might not have been the right word. Maybe it's a little strong. But I still don't think you should buy life insurance unless you need it. I believe only two percent of people are turned down for life insurance. Yes, there is a chance you might become one of them, but there's also a chance you'll be in a car accident today. I'm sure you'll still drive. In life, you can't avoid all risks. If you do insist on buying to guarantee insurability, though, make sure you buy term insurance so that, for the same premium dollars, you can guarantee as much insurability as possible."

"Very diplomatically spoken, James," smiled Roy. "I'll hurry along so you two can make your golf game."

"Yeah. If we miss that tee-off time, you'll wish you had insurance," Tom advised Roy with a wink.

"I mentioned the terms *renewable* and *convertible* earlier. Renewable means that, at the expiry of the stated term, you can renew the insurance without having to prove insurability by taking a medical. It's obvious why that's important. If you got cancer but weren't going to die before your term insurance expired, guaranteed renewability would be your salvation.

"It's often a wise move when you purchase renewable term insurance to ensure that your policy sets out the maximum rate that you can be charged on each of your future renewal dates. Why? To prevent the issuing company from allowing you to renew only at uncompetitive rates. Whether those uncompetitive rates arise through company design or are caused by some other phenomenon – AIDS, for example – you won't be protected unless your policy has guaranteed future premium costs.

"Usually, you're allowed to renew until age sixty-five or seventy. This will be more than sufficient for you three, because you'll all be self-insured long before then.

"Convertible means that the policyholder has the right to convert the face amount of the policy to any cash-value plan sold by the issuing company, again without proving insurability. This feature is important in case you need insurance past age sixty-five and can no longer renew your term insurance. I doubt if any of you will have to call on this feature, but buy it just the same. It's very cheap," Roy finished.

"I feel very strongly that no company should be allowed to sell non-renewable or non-convertible term insurance. The reasons are self-evident," remarked James Murray. "There are just too many ways the policyholder can get hurt."

"Also, when you buy your policy, always buy *non-participating* insurance. **Always**. Participating policies work like this. The issuing company adds a surcharge to your premium. Out of this surcharge, they pay you *dividends*. These are not dividends in the normal sense of the word – a partial distribution of after-tax profits. Instead, they are just rebates of surcharges. By law, the insurance companies cannot guarantee the amounts of the future dividend payments. Those amounts will be determined by the actuarial success of the company. Really, a participating policy is nothing more than a way in which the insurance company gets you, as a policyholder, to share the risk. No one should buy insurance to share risk. We buy it to attempt to eliminate risk. Don't buy a participating policy!" Roy emphasized.

"Should we shop the market for the lowest rate?" was Cathy's next question.

"Yes," James Murray replied.

"No," Roy countered. "You should always attempt to get a competitive rate, but not necessarily the lowest rate. Many agents are restricted to offering only the products of the company they're licensed with. If you are dealing with such an agent, and he or she is doing a good job helping you to analyze your insurance needs and giving you other financial planning advice, it is probably prudent to stick with that agent. This may mean not getting the lowest rate. Your rate, however, should still be a competitive one. Too much loyalty can be expensive!

"It's important to note that you probably won't be buying all your term insurance from an agent. There are two other potentially excellent sources. One is mortgage death insurance. Many savings institutions now offer inexpensive term insurance that will pay off your mortgage with them in the event of your death. Dave, when you get your mortgage next year, you will probably want to buy that coverage. If either Susan or you should die, the insurance will pay off the outstanding balance of your mortgage. The cost of the insurance, often the cheapest available, is added to the monthly cost of your mortgage. It's an excellent product, but it's not always less expensive than an individual term insurance policy. Check the rates.

"A second non-agent source of term insurance is the group insurance offered through work. Cathy, this won't apply to you at this point. Group insurance can, and I stress 'can,' be a great deal. Because it is distributed to the consumer more efficiently, group insurance is often an inexpensive alternative to an individual policy. There are some caveats with group insurance, though. It isn't always better than an individual policy. Group rates are based on the average person within the group. If you are substantially younger than your colleagues, you may be better off with an individual policy. Likewise, if you are female and the group policy has no distinction based on sex. Or, if you are a non-smoker and the group policy has no distinction based on smoking. Get your group-rate quote from your company's personnel department and then get a quote from your agent for the costs of an individual policy. Go with the least expensive. It's just common sense. Also, if you leave your company, you may not be able to take your insurance with you on a convertible and renewable basis. That's not a good situation. Instead, almost all group policies allow you to convert to a cash-value plan within thirty-one days of leaving the group. We don't want cash-value, so only accept this conversion if you are unable to qualify for individual term insurance at the time of your departure.

"Also, don't restrict your analysis of group policies to the one offered at your place of work. You may be able to qualify for a plan available through your university alumni, a fraternal society, or a union. Some of these plans are excellent."

"Tom's a card-carrying member of the Archie Fan Club. Do

they have a group policy?" Cathy teased.

"I'm offered twenty-five thousand dollars coverage free at work. Should I take it?" I asked.

"Two months and that's our first stupid question. Not bad. Not bad. Take anything you can get for free, Dave," Roy replied, shaking his head.

"How much does term insurance cost?" I queried, hoping not to embarrass myself again.

"Let's look at your example, Dave. We decided that next year you'll need around four hundred thousand dollars coverage, and Sue will need two hundred thousand. Well, using the twenty-five thousand you get as a benefit, inexpensive mortgage death insurance and properly selected renewable and convertible term – I'm guessing a little – but you're probably looking at about eighty dollars a month."

"That's it?" I was amazed. "I thought it would be hundreds a month."

"No. Term insurance is a bargain, no doubt about it. And the nice thing is that, as you get older and your cost per thousand dollars of coverage goes up, you'll have less need for insurance," Roy explained. "Your living estate will be increasing each year."

"What about disability insurance, Roy? Do I need it?"

"We'll talk about disability insurance in an upcoming lesson, Cathy."

"Next month?"

"No. Next month we're going to look at registered retirement savings plans – RRSPs."

"Should we bring our sleeping bags next month, Roy? It's almost Sunday, isn't it?" Tom kidded, as we headed for the door.

"All I'm doing for you three and that's how you treat me... Oh, the disrespectful youth of today. Hey, you two should score a little better this time out."

"Why's that?"

"It's after eleven o'clock. You're going to miss the first three holes."

"Ooh, wealthy and witty. What a deadly combination," I grinned, as we stepped back out into the sunlight.

"Don't worry about it." Tom patted me on the shoulder. "By the time we get to the course, your dad will have paid for our greens fees. Now, **that's** sound financial planning!"

6
OUR RSP

"Good morning, dear friends," Roy greeted us enthusiastically. "What a fabulous day!"

"Actually, it's overcast and cool," I noted, looking to Tom and Cathy for verification.

"I'm talking about the positively glowing feeling permeating every fibre of one's being, the day after a Tiger ninth-inning comeback victory," Roy beamed.

"You're making me sick," came from the recesses of the back room, where Clyde was stewing, and brewing coffee.

"How right you are, Roy," I smiled. "On days like this, it's just great to be alive."

"We're going down to tomorrow's game," Cathy informed him cheerfully. "Sue and Dave, and Tom and I. Oh, let me rephrase that. I'm going with Sue and Dave, and Tom is also coming."

"And to think I was going to pay for your ticket," sighed Tom, shaking his head.

"On a more serious note, does each of you have a photocopied bill to show me?" checked Roy, referring to last month's ultimatum to *get a will or else.*

Cathy had the honour of handing him all three documents.

"I'm impressed," he praised us. "You three really seem determined to get your financial affairs in order. I commend you."

"Not that we have much choice," I grinned.

"As I pointed out last month, when it comes to proper estate distribution, the importance of a will cannot be overstated. Where there's a will, there's a way."

Groan.

"You've been dying to use that line, haven't you, Roy? – no

pun intended," Tom added. "I'll bet you meant to use it last month, forgot, and spent the last four weeks in a state of depression. Right?"

"Of course not, Tom. It was a spontaneous, off-the-cuff remark," answered Roy, with a wink at James Murray.

"Before we get started with this month's lesson, I want to tell all of you that I cancelled my life insurance policy," Cathy announced proudly. "Mind you, right after I told my agent, I regretted my decision."

"Why?" James Murray asked curiously.

"Because I thought he was going to kill me," Cathy chuckled.

"Yeah. Some salespeople don't handle rejection well. Did he ask you why you had changed your mind?"

"Yes, and when I explained all the reasons, he became quite indignant and said, 'A little knowledge is a dangerous thing.'"

"To which you replied?" I prompted her.

"To which I replied, 'You're right, so why don't you take some courses?'"

"That conduct is not indicative of most insurance agents' attitudes," Roy commented amidst the laughter. "As I said last month, for the most part, they're a very professional group. That particular agent was probably upset because he mistakenly believed that he was acting in your best interest, and he was frustrated when you dismissed his advice."

"Bull," James Murray snorted. "He was annoyed that he had lost a commission."

"That too," Roy conceded. "Whatever his reason, his behaviour was out of line and, as I said, not representative of insurance agents' behaviour in general. Anyway, you did the right thing, Cathy. You have to do what's best for you, not what's best for the agent. If that means cancelling or replacing a policy, so be it."

"If you want to replace an insurance policy because you've found a less expensive alternative, or because you're making the often intelligent move from a cash-value policy to a term policy, there is an important caveat to keep in mind. You shouldn't cancel the old policy until you have purchased the new one, just in case you're no longer insurable," James Murray explained from behind the sports section of the *Globe and Mail.*

"Good point, James!" Tom exclaimed. "I'll have to mention that to my brother. He's going to switch to a renewable and convertible term insurance policy and do his saving on his own."

"Speaking of Brian, how's the real-estate deal coming along? Have you closed yet?"

"Yeah. We closed two weeks ago. We hadn't budgeted very well for some of the closing costs. Actually, we hadn't budgeted for them at all," Tom confessed. "Appraisal fees, title search, legal costs ... all that stuff adds up! But everything worked out fine in the end, and Kyle and Cindy moved in last Saturday. The three of us couldn't believe all the little improvements my brother had made to the place. He'd spent less than a thousand dollars, but the house looked ten thousand dollars worth better. Things like a bit of new trim make all the difference in the world. The guy is amazing."

"Sounds great, Tom," started Roy. "It really is incredible what a handyman – "

"Handyperson," Cathy corrected.

"Handyperson," Roy acknowledged, "can accomplish with relatively little money. It looks as though Brian is the ideal partner. Did you two discuss your insurance needs?"

"We each bought a renewable and convertible term insurance policy, naming the other as beneficiary, with a face value of twenty-five thousand dollars. If either of us dies, the survivor will be able to pay off our entire down-payment loan. Now it won't cause me any financial hardship if Brian happens to die. In fact, I'm encouraging him to take up hang-gliding," Tom joked.

"Good thinking, Tom. Not the hang-gliding part, but the insurance. You're a surprisingly quick study," Roy reflected.

"What do you mean 'surprisingly'?" Tom sputtered.

"Today, we're going to look at registered retirement savings plans," Roy continued, rendering Tom's question rhetorical. "RRSPs present a tremendous opportunity to many Canadians. All of us have to save for retirement, and there is simply no better vehicle than an RRSP."

"I prefer an RX7," James Murray murmured in the background.

"Statistics show that many Canadians retire near – or under – the poverty level. In fact, it's said that over fifty percent of retired Canadians **need** some form of government assistance to survive. That a situation like that exists in a country enjoying our level of economic prosperity is nothing short of embarrassing. Nowhere is Canadians' lack of financial acumen more glaringly evident. With our aging population, and the fact that many experts now question the long-term stability of the Canada Pension Plan, it is more important now than ever for Canadians to save properly for their *golden years.*

"Let's assume a certain successful female entrepreneur was due to retire tomorrow. We'll call her ... Cathy," Roy smiled. "Let's also assume that she has been making one hundred thousand dollars a year. How much would she need to have saved to bring in that same annual income in retirement?"

"Making our standard assumption of an eight percent guaranteed return, she would need one million two hundred and fifty thousand dollars," replied Tom, without even using James Murray's watch-calculator. "One million two hundred and fifty thousand dollars," he repeated slowly, with a low whistle.

After our second lesson, I thought I had become accustomed to bandying about large numbers. However, I'll have to admit that our *imaginary* Cathy's need for one and a quarter million dollars to maintain her lifestyle floored me. "That's an astronomical amount of money!" I gasped.

"It sure is," Roy agreed. "To maintain one's customary lifestyle in retirement demands a phenomenal amount of savings. That's why an RRS – "

"Nowadays, aren't most people members of pension plans? And what about our ten percent fund? Won't it provide much of our needed capital?" interrupted Tom, whose financial confidence level was rising by the minute.

"Good questions, Tom. Very good questions. And now is probably as good a time as any to address them.

"First, regarding pension plans. A great number of people are not members of a pension plan. Professionals, commissioned salespeople, small-business owners, for example... most of the time, people from these occupations are pensionless, if there is such a word. In addition, many employees of small businesses, in fact many employees of every size of business, are not participants in a pension plan. For all those people, it's imperative to set aside money for retirement. Beside the people who are not involved in a pension plan at all, many others are members of pension plans that, upon the members' retirement, will not provide them with suitable incomes.

"Both you and Dave have outstanding plans at your places

of work. Both of you will retire to a pension income in the area of sixty-five percent of your last working year's income. But you two are the exception, not the rule. Most pension plans don't provide nearly that well for their members."

"So, you're saying that Dave and I don't need RRSPs, but that many other people, including Cathy, do?" Tom inferred.

"No. I'm not saying that at all. It should be every Canadian's goal to have an after-tax income, upon retirement, equivalent to his or her last working year's income. That being the case, you two boys will still need to save enough money to bring in the thirty-five percent difference between your pension income and your last working year's income."

"Why?" challenged Tom. "Everything you read says that less income is needed in retirement. You usually don't have a mortgage anymore. Nine times out of ten, you no longer have dependent children. Your house is fully furnished. If you've saved properly, you've stopped having to buy insurance. Obviously, expenses are way down in retirement. So, why do you need as much money as you did in your last years of work?"

This question seemed very reasonable to me, and apparently to Cathy too, as she nodded her head sagely.

"At first glance, what you said seems to be logical, but there are some flaws in your argument.

"In most cases, several years before retirement, the mortgage has been paid off, and the children have moved out. So, for many, the last few years at work are characterized by high income levels and significantly reduced expenses. In all likelihood, disposable income is at its highest point ever. Upon retirement, it's no fun having to lower your standard of living because of a drop in your income. Psychologically, it's a difficult, if not traumatic, adjustment.

"If the decline in expenses happened to coincide perfectly with the date of retirement, instead of occurring earlier, I don't believe there would be a major problem. But it seldom does. Adjusting to a fairly dramatic drop in your disposable income is not my idea of a good way to start retired life. Especially since it's a **myth** that present-day retired people spend much less money on lifestyle than their working counterparts. People don't retire and head straight to the rocking chair. While the rest of us are slaving away, many retirees are playing golf, taking up hobbies, travelling extensively and participating in a myriad of other activities that all have one common denominator – they cost money!

"Another thing you have to keep in mind is our old friend – inflation. Many pensions are not adjusted each year to reflect the rising costs of living, that is, they are not *indexed*. Others are not fully indexed. They may have a cap of a four or eight percent annual increase in benefits. If inflation were to hover at ten percent for a number of years, the receivers of non-indexed or partially indexed pensions could find themselves in trouble. Hundreds of thousands of people were caught in this bind in the early eighties.

"Also, there are a couple of major expenditures that sometimes arise in retirement that can be very costly...very difficult to cope with on a pension...even a good pension. Sadly, deteriorating health goes hand in hand with advancing age. There are any number of medical costs that can cause your financial health to decline right along with your physical health.

"And yes, admittedly, you will probably no longer have dependent children – but what about dependent parents? As I've said many times, Canadians are, for the most part, financial illiterates. You three are learning the right things to do, but many people aren't as fortunate, including many parents. Oftentimes, elderly parents become dependent on financial help from their children."

"My dad threatens me with that scenario daily," I smiled.

"Your years in retirement should be among the best years of your life. So, you owe it to yourself to do everything possible now to enable you to enjoy fully those later years. That means saving enough money in your working years to enable you to maintain your income in retirement," Roy concluded.

"You've made some thought-provoking points, Roy, but as Tom asked earlier, won't our ten percent fund take care of our income problems? In May, you guaranteed us that someday we'd be wealthy," I reminded him.

"Yes, and I back that guarantee one hundred percent. But the ten percent fund is not intended to augment our retirement income. It is our I've-made-it-big money. It's our I-can-now-do-and-buy-anything-I-want capital. A mansion on the lake, a Florida condominium, fancy cars...these are the reasons we're saving ten percent of everything we make," Roy responded emphatically.

"But surely we'll have so much that, if we happened to be a bit short on the income side, we could always tap our ten percent fund, couldn't we?" Cathy asked meekly.

"Ah, but we'd prefer not to, Ms. Richardson," Roy the Professor chided. "Ideally, if we save properly for retirement, we won't have to. Let's refer back to our imaginary professional. If Cathy retired tomorrow, but had saved only enough to give her an income of fifty thousand dollars a year, she would have two options. She would either have to live on about half of what she was accustomed to, or dip into her ten percent fund to make up the difference. She wouldn't have to dip into it for just fifty thousand dollars, though. She'd have to use six hundred and twenty-five thousand dollars of her fund, because it would take that amount, invested at eight percent, to create a fifty-thousand-dollar annual cash flow. Suddenly, our finer-things-in-life money is being depleted dramatically. For every one dollar of income, twelve dollars and fifty cents must be used from the ten percent fund," Roy explained.

"Eight percent of twelve and a half being one," I calculated.

"And your dad said you were a 'math murderer,'" Roy kidded.

"I see your point, Roy, and I agree. I'm sure these two do, too," Cathy assumed correctly, motioning at Tom and me. "So, you're saying we should save ten percent and invest it for growth **and** save enough money separately to assure us of maintaining our pre-retirement income."

"That's precisely what I'm saying. To be in truly great shape, you must do both."

"Once again, Roy, your argument makes perfect sense. Nobody could question its logic, but is it feasible? I mean, saving ten percent and saving for retirement too, could be pretty difficult! With that on top of rent, groceries and all the routine costs of life in the twentieth century, I'll be cleaned out. I won't be able to leave my apartment!"

Tom had raised yet another valid point. I suspected Roy might have a tough time answering it satisfactorily.

"As you have learned through your own experience during the last two months, saving the ten percent isn't that difficult. By paying yourself first, it is almost painless. Have any of you missed the money or noticed a decline in your standard of living?" Roy demanded.

"No," was the unanimous response.

"But now you're also expecting us to save for retire – "

"Whoa! Hold on, Tom. Saving hundreds of thousands of dollars for your retirement may sound intimidating, but it really isn't. Remember, you three have discovered the magic of compound interest. Once again, this time within an RRSP, it's going to be our closest friend. That shouldn't surprise you. But what might surprise you is the identity of another helpful, new friend – the government."

"It's no friend of mine, Roy," Tom insisted. "I give it a hefty portion of everything I make, and in return it loses my mail."

"In the case of RRSPs, it really is your friend," Roy assured him. "As you'll see in a minute, the government subsidizes your RRSP contributions, in some cases by almost fifty percent. In addition, it allows funds within your RRSP to grow tax-free until they are withdrawn. This is a fantastic benefit.

"Between the government assistance and the savings that you will realize by purchasing term insurance instead of cash-value insurance, your RRSP contributions will be largely financed without you having to do any additional saving. You will have to do some, of course, but it will be a reasonable amount. And if we use our old trick of paying ourselves first, we'll hardly notice it. True?" Roy directed to Jimmy, James Murray and Clyde.

"True," the trio pronounced solemnly.

"How exactly does the government subsidize contributions?" I questioned.

"All in good time, Dave...all in good time. First, let me explain exactly what an RRSP is.

"Knowledgeable people have long realized that they must save for their retirements. Retirement savings plans, RSPs, have been a part of financial planning for hundreds of years. Saving some of today's income to provide for tomorrow's needs is essential, and not new. Unfortunately, statistics have shown over and over that most Canadians believe that, somehow, the financial element of retirement will take care of itself. Many others, who do understand the importance of saving for retirement, do not have the discipline to set aside money accordingly. That's understandable. It's not easy for people in their twenties, thirties, or even their forties, to worry about life in their late fifties and sixties. It seems so far away.

"Years ago, the government realized that it was faced with not only an undisciplined and somewhat uninformed work force, but also with a rapidly aging population. Clearly, something had to be done. And, say what you will about our government, in the 1950s it did something very creative and very wise to motivate people to save for retirement. It added a second R to RSP. R for Registered. If you register your plan and follow the government's rules and guidelines, you are allowed to deduct your registered savings from your taxable income, and all the money within your RRSP is allowed to grow tax-free until withdrawn. An inspired idea!

"Let's say Dave contributes a thousand dollars to his RRSP this year. That thousand dollars is deducted from his taxable income, meaning, with his *marginal tax rate* being approximately forty percent, that he will get back four hundred dollars in the form of tax savings. He will have one thousand in his RRSP, but will be only six hundred out of pocket."

"What's a marginal tax rate?" I asked, hoping Tom wouldn't show me up by answering.

"It's the percentage that is paid to Revenue Canada of the last dollar you make in a year. It's a very important term to understand. If Joe Blow makes forty thousand dollars during a calendar year and pays ten thousand in taxes, his *absolute tax rate* is twenty-five percent. However, his marginal tax rate is substantially higher. It's the rate of tax he would pay on his next dollar of income or, to look at it another way, the rate at which he would avoid taxes if he reduced his taxable income by a dollar," Roy explained.

"So, if you're in the highest marginal tax bracket, the government subsidizes almost half of your contribution," Cathy pointed out.

"With the new tax reform, not half, but yes, almost. It re–"

"I'm going to contribute as much as I can afford," an excited Tom interjected.

"There are limits on how much you can contribute annually, Tom," cautioned an apparently well-informed Cathy.

"That's right, Tom," Roy concurred. "There's a limit to our government's unprecedented generosity. They have tried, and I think, for the most part, have succeeded in developing contribution limits that, one, offer a solid incentive to save without devastating the government's tax revenues, and two, take into account a potential contributor's pension involvement. Obviously, someone who is not involved in a pension plan is going to have to save more for retirement through an RRSP than someone who is. Similarly, someone making twenty-five thousand dollars a year is not going to have to save as much to maintain his or her lifestyle in retirement as is someone who makes a hundred thousand a year. The limits reflect all of this."

"What are the limits?"

"If you are a member of a registered pension plan to which your employer makes a contribution during the year, or a member of a deferred profit-sharing plan to which you or your employer makes a contribution, your current annual limit is thirty-five hundred dollars or twenty percent of your earned income, whichever is less, minus the amount you contributed to the pension plan during the year.

"If you are self-employed like Cathy here, or if you're an employee who does not fit the description I just gave, your annual contribution limit is seventy-five hundred dollars or twenty percent of your earned income, again, whichever is less."

"Gee, I won't be able to contribute very much," I realized. "I have more than two thousand dollars coming off my pay now to go toward my pension. I can probably put in only around fourteen hundred dollars."

"I can put in seventy-five hundred," Cathy stated triumphantly.

"I'm in the same boat as you, Dave," Tom noted. "Because of my pension contributions, I'll be able to put less than two thousand dollars into an RRSP."

"But look, it all makes sense, doesn't it?" Roy broke in. "Cathy can, and should, put in a lot more than you two, because she'll need more money to maintain her lifestyle, and she doesn't have your excellent pension incomes to look forward to."

"Aren't the limits about to change?" asked Cathy.

"Yes. If the government can get its act together, the limits will be revised sometime within the next couple of years. Whenever they come into effect, it will be a big change. The proposed new limit for you two boys would be eighty-five hundred dollars a year, or eighteen percent of your earned income, whichever is less, minus a *pension adjustment*. That pension adjustment will be determined by Revenue Canada, based on information supplied by your employer. It will depend on the type of pension plan you belong to, the pension benefits to be received, and the amounts contributed. If you are self-employed, or not a member of a registered pension plan or of a deferred profit-sharing plan, you will be able to contribute eighty-five hundred a year or eighteen – "

"Percent of your earned income, whichever is less," we mimicked Roy.

"Each year after the new limits are introduced, the base figure will be increased by a thousand dollars to a maximum of fifteen thousand five hundred. And, when the new limits are brought in, you will be allowed to carry forward the unused portion of each year's allowable RRSP contribution for a period of seven years," Roy finished.

"That will help! Some years, it might be tough for people who can contribute as much as Cathy to find the money," I sympathized.

"Perhaps," Roy mused, "but I hope people don't overuse the *carry-forward* provision. It's important to get the money into the RRSP as soon as possible, so it can grow tax-free."

"Plus, if it's tough to find ten thousand one year, it may be even harder to find twenty thousand the next," Tom reasoned, as I got down from Roy's chair.

"It will be hard for you to save all that money each year, sis."

"Dave, I can see why – " Roy began.

"Can I field that one, Roy?" Cathy asked eagerly. "I had the same reservations myself, Dave, when I decided at the beginning of last year to contribute to my limit of seventy-five hundred. But, because the government subsidized me for around half of the needed amount, my out-of-pocket expenses were only around three hundred and ten dollars a month. That may sound like a lot, but bear in mind two things: One; I must humbly remind you that I make a very good income. Two; I didn't have any money coming off my pay-cheque each month for a pension. To top it all off, I had the money go directly from my bank account to my RRSP each month. I paid myself first, and I barely missed it. That's why it didn't come as any surprise to me when the same held true for my ten percent savings."

"Beautiful, intelligent, witty, and soon to be very wealthy...I wish I were young again," Roy complimented her.

"You know, Roy, Tom and I put more and more into our pensions each year. Soon we won't be able to contribute to an RRSP at all," I griped.

"A very important point, Dave. For precisely that reason, it is crucial that you start contributing now, while you still can.

A fourteen-hundred-dollar contribution will generate an approximate tax saving of five hundred and fifty dollars. So, your out-of-pocket costs are only eight hundred and fifty dollars – around seventy dollars a month. That's not too much to ask. In fact, by buying the proper type of insurance, you're saving far more than seventy dollars a month. Tom, your contribution is also very affordable – and equally critical.

"In addition to the fact that, in a few years, you won't be able to contribute, there's another compelling reason to start now," Roy continued.

"Compound interest," Tom anticipated him.

"Compound interest, indeed," an impressed Roy confirmed. "As I said two months ago, time can be your greatest ally. The combination of time and compound interest is more powerful than a locomotive, a nuclear reaction, or even a Kirk Gibson home run. John D. Rockefeller often spoke of the magic of compound interest. He once said, 'If you want to become really wealthy, you must have your money work for you. The amount you get paid for your personal effort is relatively small compared with the amount you can earn by having your money make money.' He knew whereof he spoke.

"Two twenty-two-year-old twins decide to start saving for retirement," Roy offered as an example. "One opens an RRSP, invests two thousand dollars a year for six years, and then stops. His RRSP compounds at twelve percent a year. The second twin procrastinates and doesn't open an RRSP until the seventh year – the year his brother stopped. He then contributes two thousand a year for thirty-seven years. He, too, earns a rate of twelve percent a year. At age sixty-five, they go out for dinner to compare their RRSP holdings. The second twin, who is fully aware that his brother stopped contributing thirty-seven years earlier, is confident that his RRSP will be worth at least ten times as much. What do you think, Cathy?"

"I think he's wrong ... or you wouldn't be telling us the story," was her clever rationale.

"Yeah, yeah," laughed Roy. "At age sixty-five, they would both have approximately one million two hundred thousand dollars."

Despite Cathy's glib response, the significance of Roy's point was not lost on any of us. It was a vivid example of the effect of compound interest and hard-hitting testimony to the benefits of starting one's RRSP early.

"Let's move on to the different investment options – "

"I just have one quick question, Roy," I interrupted. "A number of the people I work with never started an RRSP and now, because of the amount they are putting into their pensions, they aren't allowed to contribute. How should they save for their retirement so they can maintain their income?"

"Good question, Dave. The answer is simple. They should save more than ten percent of their income. Not a lot more, but more...say, fifteen percent. Upon retirement, one-third of their ten percent fund should be used to augment their income," was his concise answer.

"You mean their fifteen percent fund," I corrected him.

"Right you are," Roy acknowledged. "Now, on to investing. There are a number of different ways you can invest your RRSP contributions. Eligible investments include cash, Canada Savings Bonds, Treasury Bills, Canadian corporate and government bonds, guaranteed investment certificates, shares listed on prescribed Canadian stock exchanges, mutual funds that fulfill content qualifications, and even your own mortgage. In addition, you can hold certain foreign investments, as long as ninety percent, on a cost basis, of all property held in your RRSP is Canadian."

"Why do we have to have ninety percent of our RRSP invested in Canada?"

"There is a huge pool of capital in RRSPs now, and it is growing larger each year. For obvious reasons, the government wants that money to stay in Canada," Roy said patiently.

"Most of what I've read says that you should invest your RRSP dollars in guaranteed products. 'Be a loaner,' as Roy would say. The experts recommend buying things like Canada Savings Bonds and guaranteed investment certificates." Cathy looked up from a sketch that she was doing of the interior of Roy's barbershop. "Right, Roy?"

Tom seemed perplexed for the first time that day. "What? I thought it was better to be an owner!"

"The experts point out that because all RRSP deposits are allowed to grow tax-free until withdrawn, there is no tax advantage afforded to capital gains. In essence, growth and interest are taxed equally, that is, not at all, at least not until withdrawal, when the RRSP proceeds are subject to tax as they are deregistered through the use of an annuity or a registered retirement income fund," Cathy replied.

Now I was confused. "Registered retirement income fund?"

"Forget you heard that term, Dave," Roy advised me, shaking his head. "You're at least twenty-five years away from needing to learn about RRIFs and annuities...and by then the government will have changed the rules dozens of times. Cathy's point does merit some consideration, though.

"Many experts do feel that RRSP investors should confine their investments to guaranteed products because capital gains do not receive preferential tax treatment in an RRSP. I don't agree. Are guaranteed investments the only way to go just because interest and capital gains are treated equally from a tax perspective? Say that you're convinced that, through well-planned ownership, you can achieve an average rate of return of fifteen percent per year. Are you going to buy Canada Savings Bonds or guaranteed investment certificates paying nine percent, just because everything is taxed equally? Of course not!

"My RRSP has averaged fifteen percent over the years. People who have been loaners may have averaged nine percent. Does it make a big difference? Two thousand dollars invested each year at fifteen percent for thirty years will become one million dollars. Two thousand dollars invested each year at nine percent will grow to less than three hundred thousand dollars. That's a difference that just can't be ignored. The point is that the rate of return and the length of time are the most important variables in the investment equation. They are, surprisingly, even more important than the amount you've invested."

Roy went on, "In the example I just gave you, you would have to invest over three times as much at nine percent to equal the million dollars earned at fifteen percent.

"The so-called experts also argue that an investor shouldn't expose his or her retirement savings to even the slightest risk. Their intentions are good, but as I told you in May, properly selected ownership will outperform loaning over the long term – it has to. And what could be more of a long-term investment than an RRSP?" Roy asked rhetorically.

"So, we should invest our RRSP money in much the same way we invest our ten percent fund," I concluded.

"Absolutely," was Roy's crisp response. "However, there are a few things you must keep in mind. Tom, real estate is not an eligible RRSP investment. You couldn't use your RRSP contributions to buy properties with your brother."

"How 'bout with my sister?" Tom kidded.

"Also, the mutual funds you purchase must be ninety percent Canadian content in order to conform to government regulations. You cannot buy an international fund unless, on a cost basis, it represents less than ten percent of the value of your RRSP. Because the fund manager's options are limited with a one-country fund, performance usually suffers slightly. An RRSP-eligible, well-managed equity fund will normally average about three percent less a year than an equally well-managed international fund. And because the fund manager's options are limited, it is more important than ever to select a proven and capable manager. Use the same techniques we talked about two months ago and, for Heaven's sake, remember the importance of a good long-term track record." Roy took a sip from his Detroit Tiger coffee mug. "Any questions?"

"Obviously, we should use a pre-authorized chequing plan again," Cathy said in a matter-of-fact tone.

"Yes. To receive the benefits of forced saving and dollar cost averaging, a PAC plan is the best way to go." Roy set his mug down and looked at us intently. "I want to make a very important point here, so listen carefully. I've cautioned you numerous times that mutual funds are long-term investments. Over an extended period, say, a decade, the economy, and thus the stock market, will normally perform quite well. Over any short-term period, say, five years or less, it becomes much more difficult to predict performance with any degree of confidence."

"But we're buying our RRSPs for thirty years, so who cares?" I shrugged.

"You will care, Dave... All of you will. Let's say you're fifty years old and you're fairly certain you're going to retire at age fifty-five. If your RRSP is invested in mutual funds, you're suddenly looking at only a five-year time-frame. What if the market performs poorly over those five years? Because you need your RRSP proceeds to augment your income upon retirement, you won't have the luxury of being patient. You know Murphy's law? Well, don't be its victim," Roy warned us.

"If I'm reading you right," Tom hypothesized, "you're saying that, as we near our retirement, we should transfer our RRSP funds from ownership, that is, mutual funds, to guaranteed vehicles."

"That's what I'm saying, Tom. Retirement is a long way away

for you three now, but promise me that you'll keep this advice in mind. I recommend that, when you are within seven or eight years of retirement, you cash out your mutual funds at an appropriate time and purchase guaranteed investments."

"What if seven or eight years before my planned retirement the stock market, and my funds, are at a low point?" Tom inquired.

"That's why I emphasize the words 'within' and 'at an appropriate time.' Once you're within eight years of retirement, cash out the funds when their value is high – when the markets are strong." Clearly, Roy was impressed by Tom's steady flow of insightful questions. "We'll talk a bit more about timing in the lesson on investing."

"Did you mean cashing out the mutual funds in just our RRSP, or in our RRSP and our ten percent fund?" I wondered.

"Just the RRSP, because that money is needed on a specific date for a specific reason – income creation. The ten percent fund can be held through good times and bad."

"Should we avoid common stocks again?"

"Definitely." James Murray put his paper down, purposefully. "I'm not in total agreement with Roy. I'm not convinced that all your RRSP money should be invested in ownership. But whatever portion is, it should be managed by a professional, not by a salesperson."

"How do you invest your RRSP money, James?" Cathy humoured him.

"Well, I do agree that the odds favour a monthly purchase plan of mutual funds outperforming guaranteed vehicles but, despite that, I still put the majority of my RRSP dollars into guaranteed investments."

Cathy's brow furrowed. "Those two sentences are somewhat contradictory, aren't they?"

"Somewhat, perhaps...but not entirely. I own a number of properties. I also own a lot of shares in an international mutual fund. I buy guaranteed products in my RRSP because I feel it makes a great deal of sense to diversify. If the real estate and stock markets go down, at least my guaranteed RRSP investments keep chugging along."

"Is your entire RRSP portfolio guaranteed?"

"No. I have a system. If the stock market has gone down for the two preceding years, I buy a mutual fund with that year's contribution. Buy low...you know. If not, I buy guaranteed.

Over the years my RRSP has averaged over twelve and a half percent a year."

"Roy has averaged fifteen percent," Tom one-upped James Murray.

"I rest my case," laughed Roy. "Over the long run, well-selected ownership will always win out. But if you do insist on owning guaranteed products, your RRSP is definitely the place to do it. With no tax being levied on the accumulating interest, even a guaranteed investment will perform well over the years."

"You mentioned you could hold your own mortgage in an RRSP. That sounds like a great idea!" I exclaimed.

"It sounds great, but it's not," Roy commented. "If you obtained a fifty-thousand-dollar mortgage from your bank, right now it would probably cost you around five hundred and fifty dollars a month. If you got a fifty-thousand-dollar mortgage from your RRSP, it would also cost you around five hundred and fifty dollars a month. You see, under government guidelines, you have to pay the market rate even if you borrow the money from your own RRSP. So, it hasn't lowered your monthly costs at all."

"But at least you're paying the interest on the mortgage to yourself," I rejoined, sure that I had made a good point.

"You're not paying it to yourself. You're paying it to your RRSP," Roy rebutted me. "And your RRSP is capable of earning interest whether you borrow from it or not. You could buy a guaranteed investment certificate, a GIC, with your RRSP proceeds and earn interest. The only – "

"Yeah, but GICs pay around one percent less than a mortgage costs. So, wouldn't your RRSP earn more if you were paying it a mortgage rate instead of it earning a GIC rate?" I persevered.

"Dave, what you say sounds correct, but there is one problem. When you get a mortgage from your own RRSP, there are a number of fees. If you are borrowing less than thirty thousand from your RRSP, you will normally end up being worse off than if you had invested the RRSP in GICs – the fees are that substantial."

"So, we should only get mortgages from our RRSPs if we're talking more than thirty thousand," I summarized.

"No. Never get a mortgage from your RRSP because – " started Roy.

"Because it's not ownership," Tom, the pecuniary prodigy, finished, as a delighted Roy patted him on the back.

"You know, Roy, despite all your knowledge and all your logic, I think I might invest my RRSP primarily in guaranteed vehicles. Like James said, it makes sense from a diversification standpoint and from a tax standpoint. Moreover, I think I'll sleep better knowing my RRSP isn't subject to any risk. I don't have a pension, so my RRSP is paramount."

With all we had learned from Roy, to me Cathy's decision seemed like heresy.

"I respect your opinion, Cathy," Roy said sincerely. "Your reference to sleeping better is well taken, because you should be comfortable with the investments you make. Even though I am a great advocate of ownership, I have to admit that if there's one place a loaner can succeed – indeed, prosper – it's in an RRSP."

Tom watched approvingly as the final touches were made to his haircut. "Where should we buy our RRSPs, Roy?"

"Mutual fund RRSPs can be purchased from stockbrokers, life insurance agents and mutual fund salespeople. In addition, many banks and trust companies offer RRSP-eligible funds. But don't forget – not all fund managers are created equal. Do your homework!

"If you choose guaranteed vehicles, as Cathy has and as you two eventually will, I believe you're best to use a *self-administered* RRSP – the type available through brokerage firms and some banks and trust companies.

"First, what is a self-administered RRSP? And second, I thought you labelled brokers poor sources of advice," Tom accused him.

"Whoa now, Tom!" Roy defended himself. "You're misquoting me. I did say not to buy stocks from brokers. But I also said that there are a lot of fine brokers and that they can be a big help in achieving financial success. As it happens, they're one of the best sources of advice on mutual funds. They're also well qualified to assist you in managing your self-administered RRSP.

"And that, to answer your other question, is just what the name implies – an RRSP where you make all the investment decisions. It's like an umbrella, in that one plan can cover all your different investments. Mutual funds, GICs, Canada Savings Bonds, Treasury Bills and even cash, can all be housed in the same self-administered plan. Instead of the inconvenience of having plans spread out at ten different institutions, all your registered money is kept in one plan, at one place.

"Unfortunately, most people are scared off by the term self-administered. They associate it with stock trading. They don't feel qualified to administer their own plans, anyway. *Self-admins* were originally designed for the individual who wanted to buy and sell stocks within his or her RRSP. But they're actually perfect for the person who wants to buy guaranteed products... And as for going it alone...no way. You're not. You can have a trusted and capable broker at your side at all times.

"There are two major factors which make a self-administered plan perfect for the person who wants guaranteed investments. One; it's the only product that can house the full range of guaranteed vehicles: GICs, T Bills, CSBs, bonds, cash...the works. You're not confined to your local bank's limited repertoire – GICs and a daily savings vehicle, for example.

"Two; your broker can shop the market for the highest rate. If you have twenty thousand available and you want to buy a two-year GIC, you don't have to accept the nine percent your bank is offering. Your broker can shop the market, locate the best rate, and buy the appropriate choice within your plan. By looking around, the broker can often come up with a rate that is a full percentage point higher than that of your own bank. In our example, that would make a difference of two hundred dollars a year. Over the years, that really adds up.

"A self-administered plan is the best way to go for the investor who wants to keep his or her money guaranteed. No ifs, ands or buts about it. The only caveat is that normally a self-admin costs a hundred dollars a year. This amount can be paid outside the RRSP and is tax-deductible. But until your RRSP holdings are worth at least eight thousand dollars, the benefits won't warrant the charge."

"Should I buy a GIC with a one-year, two-year or five-year term?" My sister was beginning to bear an uncanny resemblance to Diane Sawyer. "Where are interest rates going? Up or down?"

"I have no idea, and neither does anybody else," was Roy's honest reply. "And don't let anyone tell you that he does."

"Or that she does," Tom laughingly directed at the Richardson family feminist.

"No, a woman may be able to...intuition and all that stuff," James Murray deadpanned.

"I want to cover three more points before I let you go," Roy proceeded. "One; if you are married, always name your spouse as the beneficiary of your RRSP. If you don't, the RRSP will be included as income on your tax return in the year of your death. If you do, the RRSP can be transferred, tax-free, to your spouse's name, where it will remain untaxed until he or she deregisters the plan.

"Two; *spousal* RRSPs. These are little gems. A spousal RRSP is an RRSP in the name of one spouse, but whose contributions have come from the other spouse. Let's use Dave as an example. He puts one thousand dollars in an RRSP in Sue's name, thereby creating a spousal RRSP. He still gets the tax write-off of one thousand dollars in the current year but, when the funds are withdrawn, they are taxed in Sue's name. For people like Dave, this is a welcome opportunity to save tax dollars. He gets the deduction now, when he is in a higher tax bracket than Sue is. She pays the tax upon withdrawal in retirement, when she is presumably still in a lower tax bracket than Dave, who is receiving a substantial pension. To prevent the abuse of this generous government offer, though, there is one special rule. Any monies withdrawn from a spousal RRSP are taxed in the hands of the **contributor** if any contribution has been made to the plan in the preceding three years.

"Three; strangely enough, there are two occasions when it may not make sense to contribute to an RRSP. The first occurs when someone is faced with the choice of making an RRSP contribution or financing his or her own business. It's imperative to plan for retirement but it's even more imperative, if there is such a term, to put bread on the table now. If you're starting your own business, it may mean foregoing an RRSP contribution. Fortunately, with the soon-to-be-adopted carry-forward provision, you may have a second opportunity to contribute. That situation doesn't apply to any of you now, but who knows ...someday, Tom might open a dating service."

"I predict a same-day closing," Cathy giggled.

"The second situation where it makes little sense to contribute to an RRSP occurs when someone knows there is no chance that he or she is going to need the money later in life. For example, if you are certain that you're going to inherit millions of dollars at some point, why sacrifice your standard of living now to save for what is already guaranteed to be a prosperous retirement?"

"I don't think any one of us is in that boat," Cathy lamented, while my mind drifted to the fact that, as an only child, Sue does stand to inherit a rather large sum of money from her parents one day. Still, you shouldn't plan around inheritances, only enjoy them. I'll be making RRSP contributions as long as the limits allow.

"My parting comment," Roy smiled, "is that you three have come a long way. You're asking intelligent questions. You're applying what you're learning. You're on your way to becoming very wealthy. Congratulations!"

Cathy acted as our spokesperson. "We owe it all to you, Roy. We can't thank you enough."

"Well, as a matter of fact, you can," Roy informed us, as we paid for our haircuts. "Give me your tickets for tomorrow's Tiger game."

"No way!" Tom roared. "Nothing's worth that much! But you'll be our first guest when we get season's tickets ten years from now."

7
HOME, SWEET HOME

"Well, if it isn't Jack Nicklaus," Jimmy bellowed, as I entered Roy's with Cathy and Tom. "When did they add Sarnia to the tour?"

"The Golden Bear! This is such an honour! Can I have your autograph?" James Murray gushed. "It's for my wife, of course!"

"Did you win a trophy or something?" Roy wondered.

"Slow down, guys," I replied. "I feel like I'm on *Meet the Press*. No, Sarnia's still not on the circuit. Yes, you can have my autograph. And yes, Roy, I won a trophy."

"What club did you hit?" asked Clyde, offering me a doughnut.

"Yes, let's relive the whole event," Tom cut in sarcastically. "Hey, I've only heard the details two hundred times... It is a sunny, windless Tuesday afternoon as Dave Richardson steps up to the third tee. One hundred and sixty yards stretch before him. Water lies on the left. A bunker lurks on the right. Perils abound. Dave laughs in the face of danger, pulls out a seven iron, takes a smooth, sweet swing and...the ball rockets straight ahead...takes one small skip...and lands right in the hole.

"The crowd – consisting of Mr. Richardson and me – goes crazy. So does Dave. He doesn't just get a hole-in-one. Oh, no. He also gets a career-low score of seventy-three. And in the process he takes his closest and most loyal friend, as well as his own flesh and blood, for every cent they have. Of course, we made him buy us, and everyone else in the clubhouse, a drink. History was made that fateful afternoon. It was an honour to be a part of it, in my own small, humble way."

"Jealousy rears its ugly head," I laughed.

"When are you heading back to Kitchener, Jack? For that matter, when's Mrs. Nicklaus due?" Roy inquired.

"We leave Monday. I can't believe that five weeks have come and gone," I answered, shaking my head. "Sue's due in sixteen days – September fifth, to be exact."

"You must be getting pretty excited."

" 'Excited' is not the word. I can hardly sleep at night. Not only are we about to have a baby, but we're also going to buy a house sometime in the next month or so. Parenthood, home ownership and a Tiger drive to the pennant, all in one month. Unbelievable!

"You know, it's funny. I'm more nervous about buying a house than I am about being a father. How hard can changing diapers be? It's the thought of borrowing eighty thousand dollars that makes me a little queasy."

"C'mon, Dave. People say buying a house is the smartest thing they've ever done...the best investment of their life," Tom consoled me.

"You'll never regret buying a house, Dave. I'll guarantee it," James Murray affirmed confidently.

"It's true," Cathy agreed. "You know what they say, 'Renting is like throwing your money away.' "

"What a coincidence! Home ownership is today's subject. Actually, it's not such a coincidence," Roy admitted. "I was going to discuss saving and the use of credit, but I don't see any harm in delaying that until next month.

"Let me start by saying that whoever the ubiquitous 'they' are who say 'renting is like throwing your money away' aren't accurate. I've read that opinion in several well-known financial planning guides, and I just don't know where the authors are coming from. Paying rent is no more throwing your money away than is buying food or clothing. You need shelter. It's one of the three basic necessities of life. Renting is one way to acquire that shelter and, in some cases, it's a very intelligent way.

"I'll let you in on another secret. The reason that the vast majority of homeowners say that their house is the best investment that they've ever made is simple – it's usually the only investment that they've ever made. My customers are always saying to me, 'Yep, Roy, my house is the best investment the wife and I have ever made.' I ask them, 'What else have you invested in?' 'Hmm,' they reply, 'we bought some old stamps one time...oh, and a stock on the Alberta exchange.' I'm sure you get my drift. The fact – "

"Hold on, Roy," I interrupted. "You're not trying to tell us that you don't believe in home ownership, are you? I've never heard of anyone who lost money through home ownership. And you get to live there rent-free, too."

"No, Dave, I'm not saying that I don't believe in home owner-ship. But I am saying that there are some widely held misconceptions about the investment merits of owning a home. Do I believe you should own a home, Dave? Yes. But do I believe everyone should own a home? No!

"As I said a moment ago, along with food and clothing, shel-ter is one of life's three *essentials*. Everyone needs shelter and it can be obtained in only two ways – you can rent it, or you can own it."

"I want to own," I interjected emphatically. "Mom and Dad bought our house thirty years ago for fifteen thousand dollars. Today it's worth over a quarter of a million. That's pheno-menal!"

"What rate of return does that represent?" Roy asked me.

"I don't know. It's grown over fifteen-fold in thirty years. It must be a pretty high rate of return," I reasoned.

"Ten percent, almost exactly. A ten percent average annual compound rate of return. Is that phenomenal?" Roy ques-tioned.

"No, I suppose not. But they also got to live there rent-free all those years," I pointed out.

"Now you're getting to the heart of the matter, Dave. How much of a down payment did your parents make?"

"I remember Dad telling me that they put down twenty-five percent. So, that's ..."

"Thirty-seven hundred and fifty dollars," Tom rescued me.

"Leaving them a mortgage of eleven thousand two hundred and fifty dollars. The monthly payment on that mortgage would have been approximately equal to what it would have cost them to rent a similar home," stated Roy.

"So, in reality," he continued, "they didn't turn fifteen thou-sand dollars into a quarter of a million. They turned thirty-seven hundred and fifty dollars into a quarter of a million."

"You've lost me," Cathy confessed, shaking her head.

"Your parents only invested three thousand seven hundred

and fifty dollars of their own money. The rest was borrowed. And, although they obviously had to pay the money back, the costs of doing so were roughly equal to what their rent would have been had they been tenants in the same house – meaning that buying the house really only cost them the down payment. Their monthly mortgage cost was not much different from what their rent would have been.

"Look at Tom's real-estate deal. The place cost seventy-seven thousand dollars, with the mortgage being for fifty-seven thousand. The monthly mortgage payment, including taxes, is around six hundred and seventy dollars. That amount is being covered by the rent. Therefore, Tom and his brother's only cost is the down payment.

"Your own home is really no different, except you are your own tenant. Your mortgage costs are being covered by your own rent...rent you would have had to pay anyway," Roy concluded.

"You're saying that our parents didn't turn fifteen thousand dollars into two hundred and fifty thousand; they turned three thousand, seven hundred and fifty dollars into two hundred and fifty thousand. Right?" I repeated Roy's earlier statements to confirm my understanding.

"Precisely, Dave," Roy nodded. "And that represents an average annual compound return of...almost exactly fifteen percent." Roy's answer was aided by James Murray's trusty watch-calculator.

"Is that all?" queried Cathy.

"Is that all?" Roy echoed, with a look of dismay.

"I didn't mean it that way," Cathy defended herself. "I realize fifteen percent is a great rate of return. It's just that I thought it would take a lot more than a fifteen percent return to turn three thousand seven hundred and change into a quarter of a million over thirty years."

"The magic of compound interest never ceases to amaze," Jimmy said absent-mindedly, as he gazed at August's centre-fold. Seeing us staring at him, he blushed and muttered, "Interesting article."

"That's a fantastic rate of return, Roy," Tom resumed, after looking over Jimmy's shoulder appreciatively. "Especially since it's tax-free, isn't it? And the whole time that you're making all that money, you get to enjoy living in the comfort of your own home. No wonder people say their house is the best investment they've ever made!"

"Your points are well taken, Tom," Roy began. "Your principal residence, that is, the home you own and in which you live, can be sold without triggering any tax liability."

"Could my wife and I each own a house and – "

"Nice try, Dave, but no. Since 1981, each family is allowed only one principal residence at a time."

"I guess my property doesn't qualify," Tom surmised.

"That's right, because you don't live in it," Roy concurred.

"The tax-free status of your principal residence when you sell it does indeed make it an appealing investment. That benefit, combined with real estate's finest quality – *leveragibility* – makes owning your own home unbeatable," James Murray stated in a very matter-of-fact tone.

"Leveragibility?" Cathy and I said simultaneously.

"That's an investment term coined by one of the finest financial minds of our time – me. Leveragibility applies to an investment that has not only the ability to be leveraged, that is, to be borrowed against, but also has the ability to produce an income to offset the costs of being leveraged. You see, not only can you borrow against the value of your real-estate property, that is, mortgage it, you can usually cover the costs of that borrowing from the rental income. It's that leveragibility that makes real estate the greatest investment of all time," replied a very convincing James Murray.

"I really think you should be on late-night TV flogging seminar kits, James," Roy laughed. "I do agree that 'leveragibility,' as you call it, is the reason that real estate is such an attractive investment. As I showed with our earlier examples, the fact that rental income can offset borrowing costs means that a relatively small investment, the down payment, can grow dramatically even if real-estate values only grow by ten percent a year...or even if they grow by less than that."

"If you had purchased a house in Kitchener two years ago, Dave, for one hundred thousand dollars, today it would probably be worth one hundred and twenty-five thousand – up twenty-five percent in two years. Not bad. But remember, you only put twenty-five thousand down, so that twenty-five-thousand-dollar increase in your home value represents a one hundred percent return on your investment. Your mortgage payments are covered by the rent – whether it's you paying the rent, or a tenant."

It's not hard to see why James Murray does so well in business. He believes in what he's selling.

"Leveragibility, tax-free status on sale, and the joys of owning your own home – why would anybody rent? Here's an even better question: why am I renting?" Tom wondered aloud.

"Despite everything we've said, there are some legitimate reasons for renting, Tom," Roy assured him. "For some people, it may well be better to rent than to own.

"There was one iffy assumption in our previous examples, but none of you picked up on it. When I was speaking of your parents' monthly mortgage payment, I said that it would have been approximately the same as the cost to rent a similar home. James and I maintained that assumption of equality between a mortgage payment and rent throughout our other examples. The prob – "

"I see it," Tom leapt in. "I definitely see it! You've assumed that the place you choose to rent will be similar to the residence you choose not to buy. That may not be the case. In fact, it rarely is the case. Look at me. I'm not about to rent a two-bedroom house. My apartment is more than sufficient."

"You seem to be developing an excellent financial mind, Tom," Roy said sincerely. "Do you two understand the significance of his comment? For a lot of individuals, the assumption that a potential mortgage payment will equal their cost in rent is a false one. Tom's case epitomizes the situation in which many single people find themselves. They're looking at rent of four hundred and fifty dollars, or a mortgage payment of eight hundred and fifty dollars. Suddenly, *renting versus buying* is no longer *apples versus apples*. Yes, home ownership still provides a solid investment vehicle fueled by leveragibility and a preferential tax treatment. But it is also going to cost four hundred dollars a month more than renting. That's a lot of money. What if Tom rented all his life and added that four-hundred-dollar difference to his ten percent fund? How do you think he would fare?"

Roy's point was a good one. The three of us were now fully aware of the power of compound interest.

"It seems to me that many single people today are desperate to become homeowners. This compulsion is the result of two things. One; parents are telling even their unmarried children that buying a house is the smartest thing that anyone could ever do. Two; the cost of houses has risen so dramatically during this decade that many single people fear that if they don't buy now, they'll never be able to. This panic is unwarranted. There are far worse things than renting your shelter."

"The hole I see in your argument, Roy, is that you are assuming people will invest the difference between the cost of buying and the cost of renting. Most won't," James Murray charged.

"I'll grant you that home ownership is the ultimate forced-savings program, and that is one of its other big benefits," Roy conceded. "You have to make your mortgage payment, or the bank tends to get annoyed. But I believe that, through paying oneself first, a renter can discipline him or herself to save some of the difference in cost between owning and renting. I say 'some' because it's not necessary to save the entire difference to come out ahead."

"Why do you say that?"

"Look at the homeowner for a second. He or she is thrilled that his or her – "

"Its?" I suggested helpfully.

"Good idea, Dave. 'Its' home value is rising but, in most cases, that increased value does 'it' little good. If 'it' wants to move, all the other houses in 'its' area are up in price as well. And – "

"Enough of this 'it' pronoun," Cathy protested. " 'It' really doesn't apply to anyone except Tom."

"True," James Murray smiled, then added, "So, what if the homeowner wants to sell, and then rent? Then the rise in value has helped him."

"Yes, admittedly then it has. But you know something funny? That seldom happens. Aging adults who voluntarily sell and then move to an apartment or old-folks' home are few and far between. In most instances, people die still owning their home. So, in a way, they haven't benefited from their homes' increased value."

Roy's argument was valid. Of Sue's and my eight grand-parents, six had died homeowners. And even though my surviving grandmother, the devoted Blue Jay fan, now lives at Heaven's Gate, she still owns her old home.

"We're not in total agreement here, Roy." This was no surprise, coming from James Murray. "I've known several people who have sold their homes and used the proceeds to augment their retirement income. In addition, the people who haven't sold live rent-free now."

"True," acknowledged Roy, "but I would argue that the real costs of home ownership, even without a mortgage, come close to the cost of renting an adequate apartment. Property tax, insurance, utilities, hydro, upkeep, and let us not forget time, add up to a hefty annual cost.

"I don't want to belabour this point. I do think home ownership is an excellent investment...one of the best. But excellent and perfect are not synonymous. I just want to inform our young friends here, especially the single ones, that renting is not throwing your money away. Look at Clyde, that slothful soul. He's rented all his life, and because his monthly costs to rent are substantially less than his costs would be to own, he's been able to spend more on other things, **and** he's been able to save more than ten percent of his income."

"Even though I do believe in real estate, I'm happy to hear you say all this, Roy," Tom admitted. "The investment merits of home ownership appeal to me, but I hate fixing things, cutting the lawn, wallpapering, and all that domestic junk. Plus, if I bought even a small house on my salary, I'd definitely feel the pinch. I could do it, but I wouldn't have much money left over for travelling and golfing...and girls."

"Yeah, your fantasy life is pretty rich," Cathy teased.

"There you go," Roy said to James Murray triumphantly. "A perfect example of someone who is better off renting. Don't worry though, James. Now he'll have more money to buy bargain properties with his brother, so you'll still make money from him."

"It may interest you to know, Roy, that with half of my commission from Tom's deal, I had their driveway repaved," James Murray bristled.

"It's true, Roy," Tom smiled. "I don't mean to blow his cover, but James Murray is a generous guy."

"Boy, James, I bought my condo from you, and you didn't even take me out for lunch," Cathy complained, with a wink.

"Speaking of your condo, Cathy, there's an example of a sound investment decision." Roy's compliment seemed to surprise my sister. "With your income, and your expensive tastes, I'm sure you wanted a nice place overlooking one of the two marinas. Am I right?"

"Yes," Cathy replied sheepishly.

"Well, there's a perfect example of a case where it was better to buy. I'm sure your mortgage costs and condo fees are about the same as the rental costs for a comparable location."

"Almost exactly the same. That's why I decided to buy." Cathy shrugged. "I figured I might as well be an owner if the costs weren't any different."

"Well, they were a little different in that, by buying, you gave up the use of your down payment. But, nonetheless, you did make the right move. Plus, you bought a condo, so you won't have to be involved in maintenance and repairs – "

"I just don't have time for that, Roy," Cathy agreed.

"Dave, you seem to be heading in the right direction, too. With a child on the way, and Sue working out of the home, you'll need the space a house provides. Ownership is probably a good move," Roy concluded, as he brushed off my shirt.

" 'Probably' is not the word I want to hear, Roy," I frowned, as I abdicated the barber chair to Tom.

"I say 'probably' because there is one time when even the individual to whom home ownership seems ideally suited, is best not to buy."

"Now there's a contradictory sentence," I noted.

"No, Dave, that situation can exist. Just ask the folks in Calgary. If home prices are about to drop, obviously one is best not to buy," responded Roy.

"Yeah, obviously," I consented. "But Calgary was different. It is basically a one-industry town. When oil went down, so did the town. Kitchener, on the other hand, is the most diversified community I know of. Certainly, in areas not dominated by one industry, we don't have to worry about real estate ever declining."

"You're wrong. Real estate can go down. In most areas, real estate has been on a steady climb since the depression, but no trend lasts forever," Roy cautioned.

"Roy, I respect your opinion, and I realize you know a tremendous amount about financial matters, but nobody I read thinks real estate is going to go down," Cathy argued. "They're not making any more land."

"The famous *finite-land* argument," smiled Roy. "Yes, there is a finite amount of land, albeit that it works out to hundreds of acres per capita in Canada.

"Look. I'm not saying real estate is definitely going to go down. But I do want to alert you to that possibility.

"Over the last several years, a few factors have combined to cause the prices of homes in many areas to skyrocket. Women have entered the work force in unprecedented numbers. Canadians are having fewer children. Both of these developments result in higher disposable family incomes. Much of that higher disposable income is being spent on housing. In addition, the baby-boom generation has matured and is fueling an increase in the demand for housing. And, on top of all that, people are no longer adverse to borrowing heavily. In fact, over the past fifty years, borrowing has gone from a shameful vice to the national pastime. Instant gratification is our society's modus operandi. The consumer-debt rate is alarming."

"Roy, you should be writing doom and gloom books, not cutting hair," chastised James Murray. "As long as people can service the debt, what's the problem?"

"As long as they can service the debt, there is no problem. But two things can happen that can lead to an inability to carry that debt. One; rising interest rates. Everyone – consumers, corporations and, most of all, governments – is in debt up to their eyeballs. Unless North America enjoys uninterrupted growth, that mountain of debt will someday lead to higher interest rates. Think about it. If everyone needs money, doesn't it follow that the cost of money will eventually go up? If everyone wants licorice, you can bet it will rise in price. Money is no different. So far – "

"The debt problem isn't new, Roy. Why haven't rates shot way up in the last few years?" Tom probed.

"Because we have enjoyed excellent economic growth. Growth that has enabled everyone to service their debts and still enjoy a higher standard of living. But, during these years of growth, the debt has also continued to grow. And each year of sustained growth brings us one year closer to an inevitable slowdown. We've always had recessions...and we always will.

"The next slowdown will lead us to the second thing that can make carrying debt difficult. Economic woes – layoffs, shutdowns, lower incomes, et cetera, et cetera. In these days of one-hundred-and-fifty-thousand-dollar mortgages, our society can't afford too many layoffs. All of you remember 1980 and '81. You remember how a recession works. Harold, the car salesman, sees his income drop from sixty thousand to twenty-nine thousand. He can no longer afford his fifteen-hundred-dollar-a-month mortgage payment, so he has to sell. But – oh, oh! Where are the buyers? Nobody else is doing too

well, either. Harold drops his asking price daily, until he finally sells his house for thirty thousand less than he paid for it."

"Whoa, now, Roy. That may have happened out west and in
a few isolated incidents here, but it certainly wasn't the norm.
In most diversified communities like Kitchener, London and
Toronto, real-estate prices held their own!" James Murray exclaimed.

"That's true. But at the time of our last recession, debt levels
weren't as high. And working women, smaller families and the
maturing baby-boom generation were not totally factored into
the prices of homes. I believe they are now. James, the bottom
line is that, in certain parts of this country, the prices of houses
have risen to the point where they bear little relation to the
houses' true value. If I were buying today, I would be careful,"
sounded Roy, somewhat ominously.

"Roy, why the hell didn't you tell me this before I closed my
deal?" Tom demanded intensely.

"For a number of reasons, Tom. One; as Cathy pointed out,
most experts don't share my somewhat pessimistic view. Two;
I don't think real estate is going to collapse. I do believe, however, that it may have a couple of down years. It's still a fine,
fine, long-term investment. Three; you bought an undervalued
property in an area that has not been subject to the tremendous run-up in prices. Four; you bought near water. I know
that sounds funny, but it's a fact of real-estate investing that
property near water seldom loses its value. Five; your brother
is capable of increasing the value of the place handsomely with
little expense. Last; you fixed your mortgage costs for five years
and your rental income for three. All in all, I think you're in
fine shape even if we do see tough times.

"The people who I think should be worried, or at least careful, are the ones who have a lot of heavily leveraged property,
without a lot of other assets backing them up."

"What about me, Roy? Would you suggest I wait to buy?" I
questioned eagerly.

"No, Dave. As I said earlier, with the baby about to arrive
and Sue working at home, it would be nice for you to own a
house. You're in a growing, prosperous city. You don't have to
worry about losing your job, and you've got a healthy down
payment. Besides – "

"Roy could be dead wrong," James Murray interrupted.
"After all, he has been giving this speech for four years and,

in most areas, real estate has continued to climb each year."

"True," grinned Roy.

"This is how I feel about home ownership," he continued, after reflecting for a moment. "For most people, it's an excellent investment. Leveragibility, tax-free gains, forced saving, pride in ownership, and reading the paper by the fireplace make it pretty tough to beat. My house is more than just a good investment. It's also my most prized possession. All I've been trying to do is warn you that it's not always best for everyone to own. But I should add, before James does, that even if you bought for the wrong reasons and at the wrong time, you would probably still fare pretty well over the years."

James Murray rose and applauded.

"Can you give me some tips on buying, Roy?" I moved on. "What should I look for?"

"When you go to buy a house, you should look at it from two angles – "

"Yeah. The front and the back," cracked Clyde.

"Good one, Clyde," was Roy's sarcastic rejoinder. "The house should fit your needs and wants, **and** it should also fill the requirements of a good investment. No one can tell you what suits your needs and wants except yourself – "

"And his wife," roared Clyde.

"And his wife," Roy chuckled, "but I can give you some tips with regard to the investment side of things.

"The age-old adage about buying the worst house on a nice street and fixing it up still holds. Location remains the key to buying any real estate, including a home. Proximity to schools, public transportation and shopping is important.

"You want to make sure that, as other homes rise in value, yours rises proportionately, at the least. To do this, you must make sure that potential buyers will always find your house attractive. The more potential buyers who feel that way, the better. Build a deck; people love decks. You'll get back your money and more. Buy a home with a fireplace; people love fireplaces. Minor cosmetic surgery will pay for itself many times over. Strictly from an investment standpoint, I advise you against a pool. Most people don't want one. So, when you go to sell, there will be fewer potential buyers – less demand. Less demand translates into a lower selling price."

"Yeah, but I'm one of the few who does want a pool."

"Then get one. When it comes to home ownership, it's more

important to fulfill your needs and wants than to make the perfect investment. You have to live there everyday."

Roy paused to look at a striking blonde passing the window. "My niece," he claimed.

"That's it?" I fretted. "No more tips?"

"Hey, buy the house you and Sue like. Assuming, of course, that you can afford it. I can't tell you what house to buy. Our tastes are a lot different. I like a shag rug on my bedroom floor; you like a mirror on the bedroom ceiling – "

"I've got one of those too, Dave!" Jimmy crowed.

"I don't have a mirror on the bedroom ceiling, Jimmy. You're weird." A change of subject was definitely in order. "What mortgage and amortization terms should I take, Roy?"

"Do you three have a full understanding of the difference between a mortgage term and an amortization term? The mortgage term is how long the mortgage agreement is binding. Among other things, the mortgage agreement sets out the interest rate, the method of payment, the penalty clauses, and the pay-down options. The amortization term is the length of time over which the debt is to be fully paid off.

"If you borrowed fifty thousand dollars to buy a home, taking out a five-year mortgage at twelve percent and selecting a twenty-five year amortization term, it would cost you five hundred and sixteen dollars a month." Roy must have relied on memory for this example, as he didn't even check with James Murray.

"For twenty-five years?"

"No, for five years. Then the mortgage term would expire. At that time, if interest rates had remained unchanged, you would continue to pay five hundred and sixteen dollars a month, and you would have twenty years left to eliminate the debt. However, if interest rates had risen to fourteen percent, you would have to adjust your monthly payments according-ly. Make sure when you renew your mortgage that you don't select a twenty-five-year amortization again. You'll never pay off your loan! You must adjust your amortization period down-ward by at least the length of the expiring mortgage term each time your mortgage term expires. Sorry, that was a little wordy," Roy apologized.

"I have very strong convictions about what mortgage and amortization terms most people should select," he resumed. Cathy, whose one-year mortgage term was about to expire, was paying close attention. "Nobody, and I mean nobody, can accurately predict the future course of short-term or long-term interest rates. There's one guy in the States who is paid hundreds of thousands of dollars a year to consistently forecast interest rates incorrectly. Just think what he would make if he were consistently right! Because no one can predict the future, it is very difficult to decide what mortgage term to take. 'What if I take a one-year term and rates rise to eighteen percent? I'll be in big trouble.' 'What if I take a five-year term and rates go down to ten percent? I will have wasted all that money.' It's a tough call.

"But James and I do agree on this point: in most cases, a five-year term is the way to go. If you know you can afford to make payments based on the five-year rate, you'll never be in trouble. Basically, you're fixing your costs and, in most cases, you can be sure your income will be rising. Sure, sometimes rates will go down and you'll wish you had selected a shorter term. But sometimes they'll go up and you'll be thankful you're protected by a five-year term. It comes down to risk versus reward. The risk is that rates may fall, and you'll be paying more than your buddies...but you will be surviving! The reward is that, if rates rise dramatically, you'll not be forced to sell your house. You'll have peace of mind – and that cannot be overrated."

"What if rates are already at twenty percent when you go to get your mortgage?"

"Good question. In that case, I would take a short-term mortgage, hoping rates will go down," Roy responded thoughtfully.

"But you said it's impossible to predict rates."

"I also said 'hoping,' not 'predicting.' If rates rise substantially above twenty percent for any significant period of time, you'll have bigger problems to worry about than your mortgage...like the guys with the guns on your front lawn. Certainly, the level of interest rates at the time you select your mortgage will play a part in your decision but, most of the time, five-year is the way to go."

"I do agree." James Murray watched Roy's *niece* pass by again, in the opposite direction. "The guy who takes a six-month term, then a one-year, then a variable-rate, trying the entire time to predict the future, is only kidding himself. Yes, sometimes, in fact a lot of times, things will work out for him.

He might well end up better off than his *five-year* friends. But the one time he doesn't, things could get ugly. Besides, some people, I swear it, lose sleep over the whole thing. They call me up and ask where interest rates are going to be in two months."

"What do you say?"

"I tell them we can't be sure where we'll be in two months, let alone where the interest rates will be," he cackled.

I pushed on, "What about the amortization period?"

"I suggest you start with a fifteen-year term. In a way, amortization is the reverse of compound interest. In the early years, your payments are almost all interest. Only slowly, as the years progress, do you start eating away at the outstanding principal. In two months, we're going to talk at length about the merits of paying down your mortgage. For now, suffice it to say that it is a very good idea...very good for your financial health. One of the best and easiest ways to do that is to shorten your amortization period," Roy answered.

Tom stared at Roy in the mirror. "Is it affordable?"

"At twelve percent, a seventy-thousand-dollar mortgage, amortized over twenty-five years, costs seven hundred and twenty-two dollars a month. That same mortgage, amortized over fifteen years, costs eight hundred and twenty-seven dollars a month. An extra hundred dollars a month will save you ten years worth of payments...and thousands in interest." Roy set his mortgage tables down beside his Tiger schedule, two invaluable documents if ever there were.

"And, because it's forced saving, it's not that tough to do," Cathy deduced proudly.

"All this forced saving is bound to get a little tough on us, sooner or later," I remarked half-seriously.

"We'll talk about saving and credit management next month, Dave. Believe me, you will make it through all this without having to hock your hole-in-one trophy," the wealthy barber assured me.

"A couple of other points about your mortgage," he went on, as he trimmed Tom's sideburns. "One; if it's at all possible, pay weekly. It really does have a major effect on your total payments. Two; shop the market for the best rate. Don't assume your bank is your wisest choice. The one down the road may be offering mortgages at half a percentage point less. That, too, can make a big difference.

"Any questions?"

"I have one. Suppose your job demands that you move every couple of years. Should you buy a house each place you go?"

"Good question, Dave. It has absolutely nothing to do with anyone in this room, but it's a good question, nonetheless," Roy grinned. "Even the staunchest of real-estate supporters would agree that, over a one- or two-year term, it's impossible to predict price movements. Keep that in mind. Also, keep in mind the fact that some of the cities our imaginary friend is transferred to may be riskier investments because they're one-industry towns. In light of all that, I would advise him to buy a property in his hometown. That's assuming it's a good time to buy, and a good city, and he can rent his property out while he rents his residence in each of his stops. That way, he will be able to take part in real estate's solid long-term growth without being subject to the risks of short-term ownership. A few oil company executives I know, who are currently sta-tioned in Sarnia, are following that strategy. They rent nice homes here, while owning houses back in Toronto. Some-times, they don't even bother to rent out their Toronto homes. I guess they don't need the money."

"They must get their hair cut here, too," kidded Tom. "What about young couples today? If I were to get married and wanted to buy a house, it would be difficult for me to afford a nice one, even with my wife's income. And it's even worse for young couples in places like Toronto."

"Unfortunately, I don't have any brilliant answer for that problem," Roy sighed. "Through proper financial planning, especially through the use of a ten percent fund, it will be possible for any couple to buy a nice home at some point in the future. I stress 'at some point,' because it could be several years down the road. If a young couple wants to buy a house soon after getting married, they're going to have to accept the fact that it won't be easy. The high prices of the past several years make saving a sufficient down payment a tough task. It means sacrificing other things – staying in on weekends; not going to Florida; doing without a dishwasher and a microwave and a VCR. It's funny, but only in these days of instant grati-fication would these sacrifices seem totally unfair. Most of us old fogies sacrificed considerably more in our early years in order to save a down payment – like cars, newspaper subscrip-tions, and good winter coats.

"There are a couple of possibilities young couples should

keep in mind. One is borrowing all or part of the down pay-ment from a relative. Parents and grandparents tend to be a little more flexible when it comes to terms. Usually something can be worked out where everybody is happy. A lot of people borrow their down payment from relatives and pay them a couple of interest points under the going rate. Obviously, this is a good deal for the borrower. Not so obviously, it can also be a good deal for the lender. Why? Because this way, most of the time no tax is paid on the interest; whereas, if it was in-vested in the bank, it would be subject to tax at the loaner's marginal tax rate."

"Isn't that illegal?" Tom asked, as he rose.

"Yes. I don't think you should do it. I just said there are people doing it. A second possibility young couples should keep in mind is the opportunity to rent out a room of their newly purchased home. Perhaps a friend needs a place and your basement has a bedroom, bath and kitchenette. Perfect! That extra two or three hundred a month could be what it takes to enable you to buy the property you want.

"It's not easy for young couples to buy a house these days. Yet, somehow, most of them manage to do it and get by just fine. I don't think this problem is new; I think it's just getting more press now because young people today think that, when they leave their parents' nest, by some divine right, they should move directly into an air-conditioned birdhouse. Ah, if only life were that easy!"

"I hate to admit it, Roy, but you're right about me and my contemporaries. We do tend to have high, and often unreali-stic, expectations. Fortunately, some of us are doing our best to learn how to not only meet those expectations, but to sur-pass them...with your help, of course," I thanked him in-directly.

"Next month?" Tom prompted.

"Saving, spending and credit management."

"Gee, Cathy could be a guest expert on one of those three," Tom tossed over his shoulder as he rushed into the street in search of Roy's *niece*.

8
SAVING SAVVY

I entered Roy's to a standing ovation.

"Here he is! The father of the year!" Roy beamed with avuncular pride.

"Samantha?" James Murray tsk'ed, while a painfully tone-deaf Clyde hummed the *Bewitched* theme song. "Were you an Elizabeth Montgomery fan when you were young?"

"You think you're kidding. That's exactly why we chose Samantha," I answered honestly. "Both Sue and I loved that show."

"Hey, guys, I'm expecting my nephew to be named either Darrin or Dr. Bombay," Cathy tossed in. "And does this mean that I have to marry a man named Arthur?"

"Clyde, what's with the black armband?" Tom wondered.

"I'm wearing it out of respect for you, Dave, James and Roy... and out of respect for your dearly departed Tigers, the once-proud ball club that was suddenly, inexplicably, struck down in late August...a sad moment indeed," Clyde sympathized, with all the sincerity of a game-show host.

"We'll get 'em next year." My rebuttal was woefully short of conviction.

"Back to a more cheerful topic, Dave," Roy rescued me from despair. "How are Sue and the baby? Everything went well?"

"Perfectly. Sue was only in labour for three hours. I myself played a major part in the delivery. I told her, 'Breathe in, breathe out' – "

"Good advice," Clyde injected sarcastically.

"To answer your other question, Roy, they're both just great. Sam is beautiful. She takes after her mother, thank God," I added before one of them could.

"Can she wiggle her nose?" wondered Jimmy.

"Everyone's a comedian," I noted.

"And word has it that you bought a house, too.

Congratulations!"

"Thanks, Roy. Yeah, it's been quite a month. We bought an older home on a nice quiet street in Kitchener. Hard as it may be to believe, we actually spent around ten thousand dollars less than we had planned to. We took one look at the place and knew it was the house for us. The previous owners had really kept it up well. It has a new roof and a new furnace. The pipes and the wiring were just redone seven years ago. We have a den, a sunroom and even a gazebo. You guys should come and see it... No, come to think of it, we're busy that weekend."

"All right, let's get started," Roy broke in. "I'm in a real hurry. I have to close up shop by ten-thirty. Marj's niece, Laura, is getting married in London. Yowza," he yawned. "Yep. I'm pretty excited about the whole thing."

"C'mon, Roy. Give and take. I'm sure Marj isn't always thrilled about everything she has to do with you," countered Cathy.

"In my defence, Cathy, I didn't complain at all when I had to go to Laura's first two weddings. But now that her *sacred* day has become an annual event, Marj's and my nerves are wearing thin...as is our pocketbook." This comment drew a laugh from everyone.

"I've got to warn you, Roy," began Tom, "I was saying on the way here that, for the first time in half a year, I wasn't particularly looking forward to our monthly trip to the barber. Your guidance on how to create wealth has been fantastic, but it's hard to get psyched up about a lecture on the merits of thrift. Don't buy fancy cars; don't abuse credit cards; don't borrow to go on trips; look after the nickels and dimes, and the dollars will look after themselves; don't underestimate the power of coupons; a penny sa – "

"We get the point," Roy put an abrupt end to the litany. "But my philosophy on today's subject might surprise you."

"What exactly is today's subject? Tom seems to think he knows. But all you said last month was that we were going to discuss saving, spending and credit management. So," I ventured, "is what we're really talking about the proper handling of our day-to-day financial affairs?"

"That's not a bad way of putting it," Roy commended me. "In this instance, by 'saving,' I mean saving for things like trips, VCRs and cars, not saving as in the ten percent fund and RRSPs. By 'spending,' I mean purchasing goods from groceries to large-screen TVs, not investing. And by 'credit management,' I mean the use of credit cards, lines of credit, and personal loans, not investment loans and mortgages. So, the proper handling of our day-to-day financial affairs is probably a perfect description of today's agenda."

"But Tom probably wasn't far off the mark with his little routine, either," Cathy speculated. "You are going to give us a lecture on the merits of thrift, comparison shopping and a debt-free net-worth statement."

"I confess that I used to espouse, in fact preach may be a better word, the benefits of those things. Historically, my lesson on today's subject wasn't unlike Tom's speech at all."

Tom asked the obvious question, "What happened to change that?"

"Nobody listened." Roy's wry chuckles didn't mask the seriousness of his response. "Oh, I shouldn't say nobody. Some of my pupils followed my advice on saving, spending and credit management. Well, at least one did. And he's certainly not in this room," Roy directed at James Murray, Jimmy and Clyde.

"After all – " Tom started.

"Let me finish," Roy said politely. "Almost everyone I've taught over the years has developed the winning habit of saving ten percent of his or her income and investing it for growth. I would guess that ninety-five percent of them have drafted wills, and purchased and maintained appropriate life insurance. They've shortened their amortization periods. They have contributed annually to their RRSPs. Basically, they combined common sense with simple, but effective, strategies to move toward all of their financial goals.

"But when it came to following my advice about day-to-day things like developing household budgets, avoiding credit cards, and exercising a degree of self-control – which is really all thrift is – generally, people ignored me."

"Why?" Cathy huffed. "If it weren't for you, many of those people would have faced bleak financial futures."

"As one who chose to ignore the teachings of a man whom he once called 'his financial saviour,' perhaps James could answer that question."

We all turned our attention to James Murray. He smiled. "Saving ten percent of your income and investing it in a properly selected long-term growth vehicle; making a will; buying the proper amount and type of life insurance; maintaining an RRSP; shortening your amortization period – these have three great features in common. First, they are easy to understand. You don't have to be a mathematical genius to grasp the advantages of something like dollar cost averaging. Second, they work. All of your financial goals can be achieved through the application of these principles. What's more, they can be achieved without a significant lowering of your current standard of living. Third, and equally important, the guidelines are easy to implement and easy to maintain. So, I was moving toward the attainment of all my financial goals, and I didn't have to study the stock market pages for hours a week. I didn't have to phone my broker four times a day. I didn't have to spend every Saturday afternoon reading books on investing. While my net worth continued to grow, I played tennis.

"Then Roy sat me down and explained why I should develop a household budget. He told me to keep track of every dime I spent, to read the newspapers each night and write down the items on special, and to save – never borrow – money to go on a trip. I remember him saying, 'You'll enjoy your vacation more, knowing it's paid for.'

"Even as Roy spoke, I knew there was no way that I was going to follow any of that advice. Drive across town to get chicken on special? – Get serious! Develop a budget and keep track of every cent? – That's just not my style. Ease of implementation? – Uh, uh!"

"Let me take it from here, James," Roy commanded. "A couple of years after I had taught James the basics of sound financial planning, we got together to review his progress. His report card read straight A's. His net-worth statement was impressive, and getting more so each day. I commended him, and myself, on a job well done. So, imagine my surprise when he admitted that he had not followed any of my advice on the managing of day-to-day financial matters! Then he told me that practically no one else had, either."

Cathy frowned in consternation. "Were you upset?"

"No, not at all. I quickly realized that, if anything, I should feel a deep sense of satisfaction. My overall financial plan had worked in spite of its users' undisciplined approach to daily saving, spending and credit management. Then I realized that it's really no concern of mine how someone manages his or her day-to-day finances. People weren't coming to me to be told that they shouldn't eat out more than once a week. They were coming to me to learn how they could eventually afford to eat out every night if they wanted to."

"The fact is," Clyde asserted, "what the hell does it matter how I spend my money if I'm already takin' care of my financial planning?"

"Once again, Clyde, you have articulated my point perfectly," chuckled Roy. "I hate to admit it, but Mr. Eloquence here is right. Our ten percent savings, RRSP contributions, insurance premiums, and mortgage payments or rent are coming off the top, that is, not being taken from whatever is left over at the end of the month. So, how we spend our discretionary income has astonishingly little impact on our financial future. As long as people are following the rest of our financial planning guidelines, how they handle day-to-day finances can safely be left up to them."

"I've got a question, Roy," I declared. "In April or May you spoke out against budgeting. Now you're saying that, in the past, you've advocated it. Why?"

"The type of budgeting I touched on in the spring is distinctly different from the budgeting I used to recommend to people like James. Nine times out of ten, budgeting that is done to create a savings fund for the future is a losing proposition. As I pointed out months ago, it's virtually impossible to budget accurately for both needs and wants. Too often, through rationalization, the wants become needs and the seemingly well-balanced budget goes out the window. The type of budgeting that I was recommending to James and others was a household monthly expense budget – a budget confined strictly to needs. To be honest, I still feel that type of budget can be very useful. It's comparable to the shop budget that has worked so well for me over the years," Roy explained.

"You see," James Murray took over, "most people, including most financial planners, have it backwards. They develop intricate budgets that cover everything from weekly gas expenses to entertainment costs to saving for retirement. Unfortunately, because most of us lack self-discipline, today's concerns receive the bulk of our financial resources. The hundreds of dollars that were supposed to be there at the end of the month to pay down the mortgage and to start up a retirement fund have shrunk or vanished. 'The damn budget's not working,' people cry. But, by following Roy's advice, we are taking care of financial planning **first**. We can be capricious with the rest of the money, or we can set aside so much for a trip, so much for a new car, so much for groceries – you know, save the way abnormal people like Roy do. It's really a matter of style. But, because you are paying yourself first and using forced-saving techniques, someday you'll be wealthy no matter how you manage your day-to-day finances.

"If a financial planner looked at the way Jimmy, Clyde and I handle our daily finances, he would probably have a heart attack. We buy groceries at variety stores. We get our gas at full-service stations. We don't pay our credit cards off every month. We join health clubs and don't go. Our day-to-day money management is an embarrassment. But we sure look pretty in *the big picture*. In fact, our net-worth statements look great. None of us will ever have any real financial worries," James Murray concluded.

I was skeptical. "You don't condone this behaviour, do you, Roy?"

"Of course not. Using some discipline and common sense, you can get a lot more out of your money than these guys do. But I have to agree that, despite their devil-may-care approach to saving, spending and credit management, all three of them are in excellent financial shape," Roy acknowledged.

"The problem is that I'm not going to have enough money left after all this forced saving to enjoy myself. I'm going to have to become a miser and a bookkeeper who budgets as meticulously as you," I worried.

"Not true, Dave," was Roy's straightforward response. "Not true at all. I realize that implementing the strategies that we've discussed sounds like a lot, but let's take a closer look. We're all friends here. Dave, what's your combined monthly take-home pay?"

"If Sue's articles continue to sell as well as they have during the last few months – she's doing well; she's on a pace to make five or six thousand more freelancing than we thought she would – our take-home pay should average around thirty-three hundred a month. As for us all being friends, I – "

"Thirty-three hundred, less ten percent, is how much?" Roy overrode me, before answering his own question. "Twenty-nine hundred and seventy dollars. How much can you contribute to RRSPs on a monthly basis?"

"This year, with my pension contributions increasing, I'll be eligible to contribute only about a hundred a month to a spousal RRSP. Sue should be allowed around two hundred and fifty a month. So, that's three hundred and fifty from twenty-nine hundred and seventy...that's twenty-six hundred and twenty left over. Our life insurance premiums total seventy dollars a month. That leaves twenty-five hundred and fifty."

"What's your monthly mortgage payment?"

"We selected a five-year term and a fifteen-year amortization period. Our monthly payment is eight hundred and twenty-seven dollars. In case you're wondering, and I'm sure you are, our mortgage is for seventy thousand dollars," was my detailed response.

"Why didn't you arrange to make weekly payments, like Roy suggested?" Tom inquired.

"The institution we borrowed from doesn't offer *weekly-pay* mortgages. But it did have both the lowest five-year interest rate and the most flexible pay-down privileges." I revelled in my newly developed ability to answer financial questions intelligently.

"All right, Dave, that leaves you with seventeen hundred and twenty-three dollars," Roy calculated. "What other expenses come to mind?"

"Property tax – a hundred a month. Car insurance – the same. The costs of running a home – insurance against fire and theft, heat, hydro, water, cable TV, phone, et cetera, et cetera – average three hundred a month. All that adds up to another five hundred. Hey, we're down to a little over twelve hundred bucks!" I exclaimed anxiously.

"So, what's the problem?" Jimmy asked.

"Twelve hundred doesn't sound like much to me," I retorted, disconcerted. "I've got to pay for groceries and entertainment out of that. Plus, I have to save for a new car and clothes and a vacation... It won't be easy," I argued.

"Look, I don't want to steal Roy's thunder by reciting his legendary wrap-up speech two months early, but there are a few points that need to be made," a very serious James Murray stated. "One; twelve hundred a month for groceries, entertainment and car expenses is plenty. Two; think about what you're accomplishing here. You're saving ten percent and investing it in a well-selected growth vehicle so that someday the finer things in life will be yours. You're doing an excellent job of ensuring that your retirement will be a happy one. You're ridding yourself, much more quickly than most people, of your biggest liability and the biggest drain on your monthly cash flow – your mortgage. Your estate planning is properly taken care of. If either you or Sue dies, the other will not suffer great financial hardship. My third point is one that Roy hasn't emphasized. In most cases, the monthly sacrifices associated with implementing your financial plan will stay level or decrease, while your income continues to climb. Because your living estate is constantly increasing, your insurance needs will gradually decline. Because of your increased pension involvement, your allowable RRSP contribution limits are also going to decline annually. Your mortgage costs are fixed for five years and will be gone in fifteen years – or sooner, if you follow the advice Roy will be giving you next month. Four;...I forget...but I'm sure there is a 'four.' "

"Four," Roy relieved him, "you've forgotten that your RRSP contributions are tax-deductible. Your cumulative total of three hundred and fifty a month in RRSP contributions should net you an annual tax rebate of approximately thirteen hundred dollars."

"It would be even more than that, wouldn't it?" Cathy queried.

"No, because two hundred and fifty of the three hundred and fifty a month is Sue's contribution and, therefore, must be deducted from her taxable income. That will result in substantially less tax savings than if it were deducted from Dave's higher taxable income. But thirteen hundred dollars is nothing to sneeze at," Roy gently corrected my sister.

"Yeah, there's that vacation you were wondering 'bout, Dave," mumbled Clyde, while he devoured what had to have been his sixth doughnut.

"Just think, Dave." An animated James Murray leapt to his feet. "Without doing anything fancy or risky, and without pinching your standard of living much at all, you and Sue are on your way to accomplishing all of your financial goals. I don't believe for a minute that living on twelve hundred a month, after all your major commitments and expenses are met, is going to put the squeeze on you. But, even if it does, remember that every year your discretionary income is going to climb. And all the while, you'll be sleeping like a baby, as your friends toss and turn, wondering and worrying about their finances."

"Now that we've reviewed Dave's family income versus expenses, you can see why I no longer feel that how people handle their day-to-day finances will make or break them. Dave and

Sue's saving for financial planning reasons is designed to come off the top, that is, to be drawn automatically from their bank account. So, even if they mishandle their discretionary income, things should work out well."

"What if Dave goes out and buys a large-screen TV with a built-in stereo? Or what if Sue becomes a chargeaholic and runs up thousands of dollars on the credit card?" Cathy demanded. "I know that their financial planning is assured through forced saving. But I don't think that means they can do and buy whatever they want."

"Of course it doesn't, Cathy," Roy agreed. "I would consider that to be the 'mishandling of discretionary income.' I would rank that right up there with the couple that earns an annual income of forty thousand dollars, and buys a brand-new, fifteen-thousand-dollar car with no money down. What they've managed to do is drain their monthly cash flow, use borrowed money to buy a non-durable good, and lose thousands of dollars as soon as their *investment* is driven off the lot. From a financial planning standpoint, that is not smart. Neither, however, is it fatal. Most people, even those I've taught, buy new cars with borrowed money all the time. It may not be smart – but I guess it's fun and, for most, affordable.

"Now, the couple that earns an annual income of forty thousand dollars and buys a brand-new, thirty-thousand-dollar car with no money down is just plain foolish. Several people in their twenties and thirties have come to me for financial planning advice. I can't believe the number of young people who want not only to achieve all the goals we've discussed, but also to own a beautiful house, a fancy car, and a cottage – **now!** They don't need a financial planner; they need a miracle worker! People must live within their means. That doesn't mean they have to scrimp and save every day of their lives, but it does mean they can't spend with reckless abandon.

"Charles Dickens's Mr. Micawber put it best: 'Annual income twenty pounds, annual expenditure nineteen ninety-six, result happiness. Annual income twenty pounds, annual expenditure twenty pounds ought and six, result misery.' "

Truer words were never spoken.

"I have two more questions, Roy," I admitted apologetically. "One of the goals we spoke of earlier hasn't been covered – the ability to finance our children's post-secondary education."

"We'll discuss that in November, in our *miscellaneous* lesson," Roy promised. "You know...November, the month you three are going to present me with a modest token of your appreciation for all that I've done for you."

"What can we get a man who has everything?" Tom asked half-seriously.

"Good point, Tom. Let's see. I've never been given a tip," joked Roy.

"Speaking of tips, you mentioned that you used to give them on the management of day-to-day finances and preach the virtues of thrift. Can you pass along a few to those of us who do want to make the most of our discretionary money? As everyone knows, it's a job requirement in the teaching profession that you be thrifty – "

"Cheap," Tom corrected me.

"I thought it was also mandatory that, as a teacher, you marry a teacher. How did you get around that one?" Jimmy snickered.

"I'd be happy to give you some tips." Roy's readiness surprised me, considering his time constraints and his earlier claim that he no longer concerned himself with his pupils' handling of day-to-day money. "It's nice to hear from a person who understands the value of a hard-earned dollar." Roy paused to look smugly at James Murray before returning his attention to me. "I won't design a budget for you or teach you how to haggle, one of my specialties, but I will pass on a few rules of thumb.

"First, a dollar saved is two dollars earned." Roy didn't just say this. He pronounced it. The shop fell silent.

"Think about the significance of that," he encouraged us, breaking the spell.

"I don't even understand it." Cathy spoke hurriedly, aware of the time. "What do you mean, 'A dollar saved is two dollars earned'?"

"Dave, if you got a two-dollar bonus at work, how much more would you take home?"

"It was Cathy who didn't understand, Roy, not me," I refreshed his memory. "I'd take home a little more than a dollar. By the time all my deductions had come off, almost half my bonus would be gone. Taxes, pension contributions, unemployment insurance, Canada Pension Plan, union dues...they all add up."

"They sure do," Roy agreed. "A two-dollar raise often translates into only a one-dollar increase in disposable income...the same increase that would result from saving a single dollar.

"If, by buying at a liquidation sale, Tom saves two hundred dollars on the price of a VCR, it amounts to pretty much the same thing as getting a four-hundred-dollar bonus. Many people would work overtime on a holiday weekend to earn a four-hundred-dollar bonus, but those same people can't be bothered to spend three hours comparison shopping. It doesn't make sense! To be called cheap is an insult – it implies a mean and petty approach to money. What some people don't realize is that to be called thrifty is a compliment – it implies a disciplined, economical and common sense approach to money. It certainly was a virtue during the depression, when I was young! Food for thought, isn't it?"

Even James Murray, Jimmy and Clyde, the resident spendthrifts, clearly appreciated Roy's point.

"Credit cards are an anathema to well-managed finances," was Roy's second pronouncement. "We all know that if we don't pay off our debt the month it is incurred, it's subject to exorbitant rates of interest. The rate on credit-card debt is often five or six percentage points higher than on standard consumer loans – so don't carry any! If you can't pay off your balance, borrow from the bank, pay off the credit-card company, and owe the bank the money. Their interest rate will be much lower."

"As long as you pay your cards off promptly, they're a pretty good deal, though, right? One month interest-free plus the convenience." CCC, Credit-Card Cathy, desperately wanted Roy's approval.

She was in for a disappointment. "Actually, no. For most people, they're not a good deal. The convenience that you view as an attribute can combine with human nature to form a destructive force, especially in the hands of someone who loves to shop. How many times have you bought something with your credit card that you wouldn't have bought if you'd had to pay cash? And isn't it usually something that you know you could live without? Then how many times have you opened your credit-card bill, clutched your throat, and shrieked, 'Five hundred dollars! What the heck did I spend it on?' So, the fact is that many people who pay off their balance each month are still hurt by their use of credit cards."

"That's me." Tom shook his head ruefully. "I never paid one

red cent in interest to a credit-card company, but I still cut up my cards last year. Plainly stated, I was abusing the privilege."

"I have to give you credit, Tom – no pun intended," Cathy sighed. "I should do the same... but I don't want to hurt the Canadian economy." I wasn't sure sis was kidding.

"Many people 'abuse the privilege,' as our friend here so aptly put it. At least you know yourself well enough to admit it, Tom. Credit cards do offer short-term, interest-free financing, and convenience, but they are not for the undisciplined," Roy summarized.

"Shouldn't we try to avoid consumer debt altogether, not just credit-card debt?"

"Theoretically, yes. I say 'theoretically' because, in some cases, taking on consumer debt can work to the borrower's advantage. But I'll get back to that in a minute.

"If you see a compact disc player that you simply have to have, what's the best way to save for it?" the wealthy barber continued.

"By paying yourself first," Cathy ventured.

"Yeah, by using forced saving," Tom concurred. "It doesn't really matter whether you're saving for retirement or saving for a compact disc player. The most effective way to do it is by paying yourself first."

"Absolutely correct! So, if Dave, for example, wants that player, he should arrange to have so much a month come directly off his pay-cheque and go into his account at the teachers' credit union. When he has accumulated enough, he will withdraw the funds and buy the CD player. Tom hit the nail on the head when he said that it doesn't matter whether you're saving for retirement or for a luxury item – pay yourself first! The only difference is how you invest the savings. It doesn't take long to save for a consumer item or a trip. For that reason, you must invest the savings conservatively. Mutual funds, real estate, and stocks are not appropriate vehicles for these savings. They offer too uncertain a short-term return. The money should be placed in a competitive, guaranteed investment.

"What I mean by 'competitive' is probably best illustrated by an example. Let's say Cathy is saving up for a car that costs twenty-three thousand dollars. After one year, she's saved ten thousand dollars...not an impossible feat on her enviable income. She's confident that she'll be able to save a thousand a month in the second year. How should she invest the ten thousand she's already accumulated? Well, she knows she's not going to need it for a year, so instead of settling for the low rates that savings accounts pay, she should buy a one-year guaranteed investment certificate. She should purchase the GIC from a trust company or bank that is covered by Canada Deposit Insurance and that offers a good rate. Don't settle for whatever rate your own bank is offering – shop the market. What I'm really saying is that investing this type of savings should be governed by one thing – common sense."

"Earlier, you said that taking on consumer debt can sometimes work to the borrower's advantage," Tom recalled. "When is that true?"

"Can any of you tell me?" Roy challenged us.

"I can!" Cathy had waited a long time to vindicate her passion for plastic. "Debt is the ultimate forced-saving plan. You have to make your payments or...or – "

"Or you're in big trouble," Tom helped out.

"Precisely," Roy smiled. " 'The ultimate forced-saving plan' is an excellent way to phrase it, Cathy. There's no way a spend-thrift like James would ever have saved up enough money to buy that beautiful boat of his – he doesn't have the discipline. By borrowing, he forced himself to save...after purchase, mind you, but still he had to save. And he could enjoy his acquisition in the meantime." For once, James Murray chose not to disagree or expand upon a point.

"I'm not suggesting that every time you want something you go out and borrow the money you need to buy it...Cathy," Roy said pointedly. "Sooner or later, you would end up in bankruptcy court. And, not only can excessive borrowing tap your cash flow, it can also cause stress. You'll find sleep comes more easily when you're earning interest than when you're paying it.

"Another thing that bothers me about *borrow-to-buy* is that you miss out on the feeling of satisfaction that comes from saving up to buy something you really want. Today, some young adults have **never** experienced that feeling of deferred gratification. They have borrowed to buy literally every major asset they have – from their TVs to their cars to their homes."

"There's a lot of truth in what you're saying, Roy," I chimed in. "Sue and I saved for three years to buy our car outright, and it gave us a tremendous feeling. I honestly think that we enjoy the car more because we know it's fully ours."

"Sure. Because, while borrowing does have the advantage of forcing you to save, it also has the disadvantages we named earlier. Live within your means!" Roy cautioned us again, while trimming Tom's bangs at a record *clip*.

"I have one question, Roy, and once you've answered it, I promise I'll get these two guys out of your hair."

"It's a deal, Cathy."

"Why did you used to recommend to people that they keep track of every dime they spent? That's a lot of work, and is there really any benefit? I mean, what can you do about money that's already gone?"

"The reason I advocated, and still advocate, keeping a detailed *household financial summary* is that it can be very informative. If you don't believe me, try it. Keep a detailed summary of all of this month's expenditures.

"A couple of years after I took over the barbershop, I borrowed money to buy a new car. When I summarized my expenses at the end of the year, I couldn't believe how much of my income was spent on my vehicle. Financing costs, gas, insurance, upkeep…close to a third of my after-tax income hit the road with my car. It was clear that, although I could pay all my car-associated expenses, I couldn't truly afford the car I was driving. It required too many other sacrifices. So, I sold the car and bought a good second-hand one – or a 'previously owned' one, as they like to say now."

"I've never done a 'household financial summary,' as Roy calls it, and I never will," James Murray smirked. "A friend of mine did one, though, and I have to admit he benefited from it. He went into shock when he discovered that, over a twenty-two business-day period, he had spent two hundred and fifty dollars on lunches… That could add up to three grand a year! Needless to say, he's occasionally brown-bagging it now," he laughed.

True to her word, Cathy began to usher Tom and me toward the door. "Thanks for everything, Roy," we said over our shoulders.

"I was just doing a little personal household financial summary in my mind, as you people babbled on," Tom yelled as Cathy dragged us further out of Roy's. "And do you know what I spend far too much on? Haircuts! I'm spending far too much on haircuts!"

Roy just waved.

▌9▐
INSIGHTS INTO INVESTMENT AND INCOME TAX

"Coffee?" Roy offered us, with a warm smile.

"Hell, I d-d-don't even d-d-drink c-coffee, but I'll have one," Tom replied, teeth chattering. Cathy and I just nodded our heads, shivering and stamping our feet.

"I can't remember a colder day for this time of year. That wind chills you right to the bone...You can see your breath... and in your case, Tom, it's not a pretty sight," James Murray quipped, to the great amusement of Clyde.

"What the heck is the temperature?" Cathy grimaced.

"Minus somethin'," Clyde stated authoritatively.

"Hey, Clyde, I didn't realize you studied meteorology at school," Tom said facetiously.

"No, I hate that metric stuff," Clyde fired back. We can only hope that he was kidding.

"Roy, before we get started with today's lesson, I want to tell you that something you said last month had a profound effect on me," Cathy announced.

"You mean it took five months for me to say something that had a profound effect on you?" Roy laughed. "I must be doing something wrong."

"That's not what I meant and you know it. Serious – "

"Let me guess what it was," Tom interrupted. "A dollar saved is two dollars earned. "

"You must be psychic!"

"Not psychic – psycho," Jimmy called from the back room.

"That same statement had quite an impact on me, too," Tom explained. "I hadn't thought about it before, but Roy was definitely right. Most of us will do anything to earn a few extra bucks, but very few of us will spend even a couple of hours looking for the best deal on, say, a new set of golf clubs.

"Golf clubs come to mind for a reason. Last week, I headed out to buy a new set of irons. I knew exactly what make and model I wanted but, instead of just walking into the local pro-shop and paying whatever was asked, I decided to check around. I found the same set of clubs for one hundred and eighty dollars less at a different pro-shop. Shopping around for only three hours saved me almost two hundred bucks. Not bad, eh?"

"And remember," I commented, "saving one hundred and eighty dollars is the same as earning a bonus of three hundred and sixty dollars."

"Well, in my case, not quite," Tom corrected me. "For me, saving a hundred and eighty dollars is the same as earning a bonus of about three hundred. But my three-hour compari-son-shopping effort still *earned* me a hundred dollars an hour. It has taken twenty-nine years, but I think I've finally learned the value of being thrifty."

"Thriftiness remains a virtue," Roy summarized.

"What's today's topic, Roy?" Cathy asked eagerly. "I seem to recall that October's lesson was to be on investing."

"Today we're going to cover two distinct areas, the first of which is, indeed, investing. Our second topic is everyone's favourite – income tax." Needless to say, this was greeted by a chorus of boos. "Whoa, my friends, do not boo! We are not just going to discuss income tax; we are going to discuss how to reduce our annual income-tax bills." Naturally, this remark met with a more favourable response.

"Why are we discussing investing and income tax on the same day?" I wondered. "Do they dovetail well from a teach-ing standpoint?"

"The reason that we're discussing them together is quite complex, but here it is..." Roy paused and looked pensive. "In terms of time, they each take approximately one haircut to cover."

"That is deep," Tom deadpanned.

"I don't know much about investing, Roy, but I do know that even a teacher as skilled as you can't cover all the ins and outs of investing during one haircut...not even if the client is Rapunzel."

"You're right, Cathy," Roy conceded. "To cover the ins and outs of all the different types of investments in that short a time-frame would be impossible. But that's okay, because one of the chief prerequisites of a financial plan is that its successful implementation not be dependent on expert investment management by the *plannee*. Why? Because most of us aren't capable of performing in-depth investment analysis and, what's more, most of us don't even want to become capable!"

"Amen," I interjected.

"Successful investing is elusive. If it weren't, everybody would be shopping on Rodeo Drive. Few have the time it takes to properly analyze different investment alternatives. Those who do have the time to assess the risks and rewards of a given investment must also have both strong mathematical ability and sufficient knowledge to enable them to apply that ability wisely. That might involve anything from having an accounting background when studying stocks, to having a feel for the local economy when selecting a commercial real-estate site."

"I'm sorry to interrupt you here, Roy," apologized James Murray. "But I want to reiterate something I said way back in May. Not only does successful investing take a lot of time and specialized knowledge, but it also takes tremendous discipline and an eye for value...an eye that is often more intuitive than informed."

"I would go one step further, James, and say that, without discipline and an eye for value, an investor is doomed to dismal failure. I know several well-trained, well-informed investors who consistently lose money. They lack either the required discipline or the eye for value. Conversely, I know people who lack specialized knowledge, but still have successful investment records because of their discipline and eye for value.

"Remember in May when James pointed out that, to make money in the stock market, you have to 'buy low, sell high'?" Roy asked us.

"It doesn't take a genius to figure that out," I replied.

"No? Then why do most market investors do the exact opposite? They buy high and sell low – a foolish approach if ever there was one."

"They lack self-discipline," Tom shrugged. "Stocks are low when almost nobody wants them. So, to buy low, you have to buy at just the time when most people are saying it's not smart to do so."

"Exactly," Roy confirmed. "It may be the only law that has never been broken – the law of supply and demand. When a stock's price is low, it's down for only two reasons: there are too few buyers and too many potential sellers. In other words, the stock is relatively unwanted. To buy in that kind of environment takes a courage that few of us have."

"It's the same on the sell side," I broke in strongly. "You're supposed to sell high. When is a stock high? It's high when everyone wants it. It's high when demand is high and supply is low. It's not easy to sell a stock when all your co-workers and neighbours are telling you what a great buy it is."

"Can you see why discipline, which I define as the courage to buy when others are selling and to sell when others are buying, is so important? Without it, you're just another sheep... and you're probably heading toward a slaughter," Roy warned us.

" 'Buy low, sell high' is impossible without self-discipline or 'courage' as Roy calls it," James Murray summed up.

"How about *buy high, sell higher*?" Tom suggested.

"Certainly it's possible but, for obvious reasons, buying low is a much less risky proposition. Many people have lost small fortunes buying late in a market rally, buying high, that is, because they convinced themselves that 'this time it will be different.' That fateful phrase has cost a lot of people a lot of money. Attempting to buy high, sell higher, is simply a fool's game," was Roy's vigorously stated philosophy.

"I would be worried about *buy low, sell lower*, " I admitted. "I mean, after all, aren't most stocks low just before they drop off the board?"

"True, Dave," Roy responded supportively. "Just before a gas tank hits empty, it does pass through low. That's why, along with discipline, to be a prosperous investor, you must also have that eye for value. You have to recognize the difference between an investment, say, a common stock, that's undervalued, and one that just isn't healthy. There are many unwanted, hence low-priced, investments that are unwanted for good reason. For example, you could show courage by buying a home in Buffalo's Love Canal district, but I think you'll agree that that might also demonstrate a poor eye for value."

"What about real estate? There it seems that, for the most part, buying low and buying value aren't that important. The operative expression seems to be, *buy at any price, sell higher*."

"Quite honestly, Tom, I can't put up a strong argument against your point. With the exception of some one-industry towns, real-estate prices have been on a steady climb for fifty years. Sure, during tough economic times and recessions, values have suffered, but not much. In some areas, it seems that a *bad* year is defined as a twelve-month period during which home values rise only slightly. That being said, I'd like to add the following: Most real-estate investors have enjoyed solid returns throughout the last half-century, but the ones who have exercised discipline and bought value have been even more successful. Yeah, the guy who bought an overpriced duplex toward the end of an economic boom probably did sell it for a good profit several years later. However, the canny investor who located a bargain property and bought it during a recession will have reaped even greater rewards.

"Also, and I urge you to heed my words here, in my opinion the halcyon days of guaranteed easy money in real estate are coming to an end. As I mentioned in our conversation on home ownership, no trend is permanent. There's no law that says real estate can't decrease in value. I grant you that, over the long term, well-selected real estate should always perform well. Note the term 'well-selected.' If you use discipline and common sense, and buy value, real estate will treat you well. But, I don't think buying property without regard to location, timing and value will continue to be a profitable strategy." Roy was quite adamant about this prediction.

"What worries me, Roy, is that I don't think I have the qualities you're talking about. I certainly don't have the knowledge, and I have no reason to believe I have either investing courage or an eye for value...especially the latter."

"Don't worry, Dave," Roy reassured me. "As I said earlier, one of the prerequisites for a sound, productive financial plan is that its successful implementation **not** require tremendous investment management skills on the part of the plannee. "

"I remember that point vividly," I grinned. "It gave me great comfort."

"Look at your financial plan, and Cathy's," Roy continued. "You're both using professional money management, forced saving, dollar cost averaging, conservative RRSPs, a shortened amortization, proper insurance coverage...you know, all the boring things that make people wealthy. What in that plan calls for any complicated investment decisions? Before you answer, remember that your short-term savings for things like cars and trips are to be invested in guaranteed products."

"I see your point, Roy, but what if, down the road, Sue and I have a lump sum to invest...say, an inheritance or royalties from a travel guide that Sue might write?"

"And what about me?" Tom cut in. "Because I'm buying real estate with my ten percent fund, I'm forced to make investment decisions. I don't have the safety net of dollar cost averaging."

"That's right, Tom, you don't," Roy answered, seemingly ignoring the fact that I had posed a question before Tom. "I pointed out in May that when you elect to buy real estate with your ten percent fund, timing does become an issue. The discipline and eye for value we spoke of earlier are both important and, for reasons I just explained, will probably become even more so in years to come. That's the bad news. The good news is that you do seem to demonstrate those qualities. You've bought a property in an area that hadn't been subject to the recent run-up in prices and, what's more, you've bought a property that James described as one of the better values he had seen."

"I'm flattered that you feel that way, Roy. Unfortunately, my purchase had more to do with luck than wisdom. I didn't – "

"Yes, you did!" Roy stopped Tom abruptly. "You did recognize that property represented good value. I remember you saying that, with the size of the lot, the proximity to the water, and the nice neighbourhood, the property was definitely underpriced. Don't you? James pointed out today that the eye for value is more often intuitive than informed. This is especially true of real-estate investors. Quite a few people seem to have a knack for locating potentially profitable properties. Boy, how's that for alliteration?"

"Pretty powerful," Cathy quipped.

"Another intelligent thing you did, Tom," Roy continued, "was to consult James for an opinion. His success is a testimony to his ability to spot the *right* property."

"Getting back to humble, little me," I tried again, "what about my lowly question? I don't have Tom's eye for value and, even if I did, I probably wouldn't use it. I don't want to be an investor; I want to be a teacher."

"Yes, even though our plans are designed to diminish, if not eliminate, the necessity for investment skills, there could possibly be times when you are faced with an investment decision. Your example of an inheritance was a good one, Dave." Roy stopped speaking long enough to get the attention of Jimmy, who was half-asleep. "Jimmy, if someone finds him or herself with excess cash from an inheritance, or from any other source, including savings from cash flow, what's the wisest investment he or she could make?"

"Pay off consumer debt," Jimmy shot back.

"No doubt about it," James Murray seconded.

"There is simply no better investment alternative for the average Canadian than to pay off his or her consumer debt... including the mortgage. The reasons are many. First and foremost, paying off consumer debt offers a great return on your money...not good, great! This is one of the simplest, yet least understood, concepts of proper money management. Interest on a consumer loan, be it a car loan or a mortgage on a non-investment property, is not a tax-deductible expense.That means that the twelve percent interest you're paying to your bank for your furniture loan is being paid off with after-tax dollars. So, if instead of paying off that same loan, you decided to buy a guaranteed investment certificate, what rate would the GIC have to pay just for that choice to result in a break-even proposition?"

Roy's question drew no immediate response.

"**Twenty** percent," Cathy finally blurted out. "If I bought a GIC paying twenty percent, because I'm in roughly a forty percent tax bracket, I would then earn twelve percent after tax. That's the same rate of return I am essentially *earning* by paying off my twelve percent furniture loan."

"Bravo! Do you two understand?"

Tom and I nodded our heads.

"Something just struck me," Tom said thoughtfully. "If paying off a twelve percent consumer loan equates with earning a twenty percent interest return, just think what interest you would have to get to break even with the paying-off of a credit-card debt. Some of those cards are charging as much as eighteen percent on outstanding balances. You'd have to earn a **thirty** percent interest return just to come out even!"

"Now, I ask you, is that complex mathematics? No, of course not," Roy answered his own question. "Yet, incredible numbers of Canadians who have outstanding consumer loans also own Canada Savings Bonds and guaranteed investment certificates that pay fully taxable interest. It often doesn't make any sense. Mister X buys ten thousand dollars worth of CSBs that are paying nine and a half percent. After paying tax, he's lucky if he's keeping seven percent. At the same time, he's paying his credit union loan off at thirteen percent interest with **after-tax** dollars. C'mon!" he scoffed.

"Knowledgeable investors agree that a three percent after-tax real rate of return is very good. Incidentally, what do I mean by 'after-tax real rate of return'?" Roy quizzed.

"The absolute rate of interest less the amount paid in taxes, less the inflation rate," Tom expounded. "Basically, it's the amount you're gaining in purchasing power."

"Impressive. By paying off a twelve percent consumer loan, your after-tax rate of return is that same twelve percent, because the loan was being serviced with after-tax dollars. Let's say inflation is six percent. The after-tax real rate of return becomes, therefore, six percent...twice what is considered to be quite acceptable."

"I have a question. Should you always pay off the highest-interest-rate consumer loan first?"

"Dave, it should be common sense that, if you have some money available to pay down consumer loans, you should pay down the one with the highest interest rate. Yet, many people put two thousand dollars down on their eleven percent mortgage, and leave their eighteen percent credit-card balance untouched. Yikes! Yes, always pay off the loan with the highest associated interest rate," Roy answered diplomatically.

"There are a couple of other major considerations here," James Murray cut in. "Not only does paying down consumer debt offer an excellent rate of return, but it is also **guaranteed**, and there is a zero PITA factor. Reducing debt also reduces stress, and if that debt happens to be a mortgage, eliminating it also contributes to pride in ownership. It's a great feeling to own your home, free and clear. The bottom line is that, for most people, paying off consumer debt is the best investment alternative."

"Well, I'm glad that paying off consumer debt is a wise move because it's certainly the strategy that I feel most comfortable with...no heavy analyses, zero PITA factor...and, hey, eventually it'll free up my cash flow for other things."

"That's the benefit I've enjoyed the most," Jimmy reported. "Since I paid my mortgage off, I've increased my ten percent fund to a fifteen percent fund, and I still have a high disposable income. In my mind, the freed-up cash flow is the most satisfying benefit of paying off consumer debts."

"And to think we didn't even mention it, James," the wealthy barber chortled.

"What if we reach a point where we have money to invest and we have no consumer debt?" Cathy's red face betrayed the fact that she was somewhat embarrassed by her question. However, with her lucrative income, the hypothesis was valid.

"Jimmy?" Roy redirected the question.

"Years ago, I found myself in just that position. I had accumulated several thousand dollars and I had no debt...not even a mortgage. I went to Roy and asked him for some specific investment advice. You won't believe what he told me to do. 'Spend the money!' He told me to spend it! Now, that's my type of financial planner," Jimmy concluded, giving Roy the thumbs-up sign.

"His fifteen percent fund was growing nicely, as was his RRSP. He had no debt. He had no need for life insurance. His daughter's education was secure. In short, all his financial goals were being met. I suggested that he go out and buy something he'd always wanted... a toupee perhaps."

Roy's advice to Jimmy didn't surprise me at all. In April, Roy had stressed that a well-designed financial plan should meet our future goals without dramatically lowering our current standard of living. In view of that, Roy's suggestion to "spend it" made perfect sense. Why shouldn't people live to the fullest once their financial futures are well taken care of?

"If you find yourself in the enviable position of having more money than you care to spend, I strongly recommend that, rather than investing it all at once, necessitating a correct investment decision, you spread out the investment by increasing your ten percent fund monthly savings. Let's say you had an extra five thousand dollars. Put two hundred dollars more each month into your pre-authorized chequing plan. Obviously, the five thousand will eventually run out, and then you'll have to revert to your normal monthly saving amount. In the meantime, though, you will have invested your money wisely, taking advantage of the same strategies we've discussed before and, once again, you will have avoided having to time an investment purchase precisely."

It was hard for me to get excited about Roy's last bit of advice. Although I'm sure that I'm now on the road to financial prosperity, the point at which I will have more money than I care to spend is still years away.

Roy whisked me off as I stepped down from the barber chair. "On to income taxes?" I anticipated.

"I have a question first," Tom slowed us down. "Don't we ever get to buy a penny stock or something that's fun like that?"

"Mark Twain once wrote, 'There are two times in a man's life when he should not speculate: when he can't afford it, and when he can.' If you want to play the market, buy commodities, or buy options on gold, don't do it under the guise of financial planning. Yes, it can be fun. Yes, it can be exciting and, yes, very occasionally, it can be profitable. The same things can also be said of a trip to Las Vegas. And, I should add, Las Vegas serves free drinks and is full of long-legged showgirls. Go to Vegas." Roy does have an effective way of driving a point home.

"Before we move on to income taxes, I want to share an idea that came to me the other day...an excellent idea," James Murray started modestly, as he set aside the real-estate section of the paper. "As you know, the only piece of Roy's financial planning advice that I've chosen not to follow is his recommendation to place RRSP dollars in ownership investments. I still maintain that, from a diversification standpoint, it doesn't make sense to have all your long-term savings in one basket. My ten percent fund includes equity-oriented mutual funds. I own several properties and I invest most of my RRSP dollars in guaranteed vehicles. In my RRSP, I'm primarily a loaner. Because the interest earnings are allowed to compound tax-free until withdrawal, my RRSP has grown significantly. Cathy, you indicated that you, too, have decided to go the guaranteed route with your RRSP dollars. And, although you two didn't say so, I sensed some apprehension on your part about having an entirely equity-based RRSP."

"With all due respect, Roy, I have to confess that James's diversification argument, combined with the manner in which RRSP deposits can compound tax-free, does make being a loaner look like an attractive alternative." I agreed with Tom, and was glad he had spoken up.

"I still favour ownership, but I'll repeat that if there is one place a loaner can prosper, it's in an RRSP... And the diversification argument has some validity," Roy admitted, somewhat reluctantly. "What's your 'excellent idea,' James?"

"First, once your RRSP is worth ten thousand dollars, open

a self-administered plan. Then, buy a guaranteed investment certificate within the plan for the entire available amount – not just any GIC, but a monthly-interest GIC. Then, open a monthly pre-authorized chequing plan with a properly selected mutual fund for the same amount as the monthly GIC interest. Instead of all the money being automatically withdrawn from your bank each month, it will come from your self-administered plan. Each year, as you contribute to your RRSP and repeat the process, alter the PAC amount accordingly. It's beautiful – all your capital is guaranteed, yet you're still reaping the benefits of ownership, dollar cost averaging, professional money management...the works. It's tidy – there are no small amounts of money left sitting idly by. It's easy – twenty minutes of work a year, and no complicated investment decisions. Essentially, what you're doing is compounding your GIC interest into ownership. It's a great compromise!"

All eyes turned to Roy. "Hmm... That is one of the best ideas for investing an RRSP that I've heard." James Murray smiled broadly. "You're right, James, it is an excellent compromise for those people who want to be loaners in their RRSPs."

I had found my RRSP investment strategy.

"So, the mutual fund shares would accumulate each month in your self-admin plan?"

"That's right. I'm not sure that all companies offering self-admins would be open to this idea, it is a lot of paperwork, but I am sure something could be worked out with some of them. Sounds great, eh?" James Murray patted himself on the back.

"Certainly worth looking into... Now on to our favourite subject," Roy brought us all back to earth. "Income tax."

"A dollar saved is two dollars earned," Roy repeated this familiar refrain.

"That was last month's lesson, Roy. We're covering income tax now, remember?" Tom joshed.

"A dollar saved is two dollars earned, whether it's a dollar saved through coupons or through reduced tax," James Murray mused. "What's more, a tax dollar saved is one less dollar for the government to spend, not one less dollar for you to spend."

"What James means by that is that, normally, to save a dollar we must make some sacrifice, but when we save a tax dollar, there is no associated sacrifice. Tax savings are savings of the best kind," Roy clarified. "Because of that, it's important

that each of you does your best to minimize your tax bill...
your legal best, that is. Tax evasion is illegal and is not recommended. In fact, the almost epidemic proportions that tax evasion has reached, through non-reporting of all sources of
income, is one of our country's major economic woes.

"On the other hand, tax avoidance, the minimizing of one's
tax bill through the proper handling of one's financial affairs,
is an important part of financial planning."

"I hate to keep playing the devil's advocate," I broke in
somewhat sheepishly, "but I have even less interest in becoming a tax expert than I did in becoming a knowledgeable investor. The mere mention of the word *accounting* makes me
shudder."

"Once again, your nervousness is unfounded," Roy assured
me.

"We have said that one of the prerequisites of a sound and
productive financial plan is that its successful implementation not be dependent on expert investment management by
the plannee. Another prerequisite is that the successful implementation not be dependent upon the plannee becoming a tax
expert." Tom offered an almost perfect imitation of the wealthy barber.

"You must have studied financial planning under a brilliant
mentor, Tom," Roy laughed. "What Tom just said is very true.
Producing and following a sound financial plan should not be
dependent upon the plannee being a tax expert, not just because becoming a tax authority is an arduous task, but also
because, for most of us, there are very few *tax tricks* that are
worth knowing. No matter how knowledgeable about the tax
system we may be, we have very few opportunities to legitimately reduce our tax burden."

"Even chartered accountants pay standard amounts of personal income tax," James Murray pointed out.

"Unless you run your own business, I can teach you a lot
of what you need to know about income tax in a matter of
minutes."

"I do run my own business, and so does Sue now. What
about us?" Cathy pleaded.

"The tips I'm going to give these two should still be of some
help to you, but there is one other tip you should take very
seriously – see an accountant!" Roy instructed forcefully.

"I have an accountant," Cathy told him, adding, "an excellent accountant...a handsome accountant. He does all my personal and business returns, calculates how much I should draw out of the business each year, creates quarterly balance sheets and income statements, keeps me informed...and looks great."

"It's **imperative** that a business owner work closely with a qualified accountant. A good accountant is worth his or her weight in gold...and most are good. The professionalism and training in the accounting field are unparalleled. Accountants are not selling products;they are selling expertise, so their advice tends to be unbiased. If you are a business owner or someone whose financial affairs are very complex from a tax standpoint, enlist the services of an expert! I can't stress that enough."

"I think you just did, Roy," Tom noted.

"Tom, you'll look great in a mohawk," Roy threatened. "What can you two boys do to reduce your taxes?"

"RRSPs," I answered. "An RRSP contribution reduces taxable income, and a spousal RRSP can be a really effective way of reducing income taxes."

"Very good, Dave. Tom?"

"Take advantage of the one-hundred-thousand-dollar capital-gains tax exemption by saving ten percent of all you make and investing it for growth."

"Excellent. Any other ideas?"

"Invest the baby bonus – " I began.

"We're going to save that one for next month, Dave," Roy interrupted me. "Aside from making RRSP contributions and taking advantage of the one-hundred-thousand-dollar capital-gains tax exemption, there are only two worthwhile ways that I know of for the average Canadian to legally reduce his or her tax bill."

"What do you mean by 'worthwhile'?" I wondered.

"Well, there are some ways to reduce your taxes that are perfectly legitimate, but often not worth the time or effort. An example – tax experts are always recommending that you defer the receipt of income to the next tax year, whenever possible. They reason, correctly, that by deferring your tax liability, you are keeping the use of your money for an additional year. If Tom's brother earned a thousand dollars on the side in December doing some trimming, it would be wise for him to request payment in January. By deferring the tax liability for one year, Brian would have twelve months to use the four hundred dollars he would have had to pay in taxes. Four hundred dollars could earn forty dollars interest...less sixteen dollars in tax...twenty-four dollars. Hey, twenty-four dollars is twenty-four dollars, but the average person is not going to spend a lot of time tax-planning for that type of money.

"I'm certainly not saying this type of planning is a waste of time – I do it. Remember, 'a dollar saved is two dollars earned.' However, for most people, this may be taking tax-planning a bit too far."

"I agree, Roy, but what if someone could defer the receipt of ten thousand dollars?"

"Obviously, that's a much different case, Cathy. The average Canadian, though, doesn't have the opportunity to defer anything close to that amount of income." Very true. Most of us are wage-earners who are happy to accept pay-cheques whenever they are offered.

"So, what are the two worthwhile ways?" Tom probed.

"The first is proper income-splitting. You don't have to be a math professor to understand that as much income as possible should be claimed by the lower wage-earners in the family."

"Hey, Roy," I blurted out, "you're not going to believe this, but I know a fair amount about that stuff!"

"You're right; I don't believe it," Roy chuckled.

"A friend of mine taught me the basics of income-splitting last year. Because I earn more money than Sue, all of our savings accounts are in her name. That way, the taxable income those accounts earn is taxable in Sue's hands, not mine. And the baby bonus – "

"We're going to talk about the baby bonus **next** month," Roy reminded me. "Your example of income-splitting is well taken. Over the years, that type of planning can save people significant sums of money."

"What can Cathy and I do, income-splitting-wise?" Tom tossed in. "We don't have spouses or children to split with."

"Get married."

"Get married to avoid income taxes...Roy, you're such a romantic," Cathy shook her head. "Then again, I wonder if my accountant would be game?"

"If you and Tom married each other," Roy showed his bias, "you could pay him a small salary for doing your books, thereby reducing your taxable income."

"Yeah, but I'd be increasing Tom's taxable income by the same amount," Cathy argued.

"True," Roy granted, "but it's the same concept as in Dave's savings account example. Tom's taxable income would be increasing by the same amount as yours would be decreasing but, because you would be in a higher marginal tax bracket than Tom, it would result in significant tax savings.

"Proper income-splitting is just a matter of using your head. It's just common sense. If Sue's earnings are lower than Dave's, then, of course, we want the savings accounts in her name."

"I don't think my father understands income-splitting," Cathy jumped in. "All of my parents' savings are in Dad's name, and he's in a much higher tax bracket than Mom. I'm going to tell him to switch that around immediately!"

"Whoa, now!" cautioned Roy. "That's a waste of time. It contravenes the *attribution rules*."

"Attribution rules?" Cathy echoed. "What are those?"

"If income-producing property is transferred by a low-interest loan or by gift from one spouse to another or to anyone under eighteen years of age, the recipient's income from that property is taxed in the hands of the donor. In addition, if an income-producing property is transferred via a low-interest loan to a *non-arm's length* party, a relative, regardless of their age, the income is again taxed in the hands of the donor. The attribution rule also applies to capital gains in a spouse-to-spouse transfer," Roy explained.

"That's unfair!" my disappointed sister groaned.

"Not really, Cathy," Roy responded. "In fact, the attribution laws are very fair. It's through your dad's earnings that those savings were created, therefore they should be in his name – and taxed in his name."

"What about Dave and Sue? You said it was a good idea for them to keep their savings accounts in Sue's name. Don't the attribution laws apply there, too? I mean, Dave is making more money than Sue. Wouldn't those savings more likely be his? Or shouldn't at least a hefty percentage be in his name?"

"Thanks, sis. I appreciate all you're trying to do for me... Or should I say to me?"

"There is some logic in what you're saying, Cathy, but no, the attribution rules wouldn't apply in Dave's case. You see,

Dave could easily argue that the money in the savings accounts was saved exclusively from Sue's income and that his income was used to pay the bills. Whereas, in your parents' case, with your mom never having worked outside the home, that argument wouldn't wash."

"What if Mr. Richardson lied?" Tom suggested. Roy just sighed.

"As I said a minute ago, the attribution rules are fair. Without them, each family could arrange their affairs in such a way that the government would be able to collect very little tax on investments and savings."

"Sounds good to me, Roy," Tom tossed in.

"It doesn't sound so good to the sick, the needy, the unemployed...all those who require government assistance. And it wouldn't be fair to future generations, who will already be saddled with a huge debt."

"You do believe in paying your fair share of taxes, don't you, Roy?" Tom surmised.

"I certainly do, Tom, 'fair share' being the key term. I have nothing against organizing your financial affairs in the wisest possible way to minimize your tax liability. However, tax evasion is a whole different ball game. It's illegal and irresponsible. What's more, it's unnecessary if you do proper financial planning."

"As Roy said earlier, proper income-splitting just comes down to using your head," James Murray reiterated. "I pay my wife a salary for keeping my books and doing all my secretarial work. It's perfectly legitimate – she really does work for me – and it's a very effective tax strategy. Out of my hands and into hers, so to speak. Another example: Several years ago, I had ten thousand dollars sitting in my savings account from a commercial real-estate deal. My daughter was fifteen, so I gave her the money to buy a three-year compounding guaranteed investment certificate. Why? Because when the GIC matured she would be eighteen, so the attribution rules wouldn't apply. The interest earned was taxable in her hands, not mine. As a university student, she had a low taxable income and ended up paying **no** tax on the interest gain. I would have paid handsomely! It was only logical to plan that way."

"I should point out a few things about James's last example," Roy added. "One; you can only use that type of strategy with a child fifteen years of age or older because the interest on a compounding investment must be claimed at least every three years. If you did it with, say, a five-year-old, the interest would be attributed back to you three years later because the child was not yet eighteen. Two; the government lost out on this manoeuvre, but so did James. If he had invested the money in his own name, he would have had to pay tax. However, even after tax, he would have made some return. By giving the money to his daughter and letting her spend the income, he avoided tax but he also missed out on earning a return for himself. Essentially, he helped his daughter out and got the government to partially subsidize his generosity. Three; had he given his daughter the money and then asked for the repayment of the principal and the investment gain, he would have been breaking the rules – it would have been a low-interest loan. Four; if you implement a strategy for the sole purpose of avoiding tax, the government may deem it inappropriate and reverse it. In James's case, he gave Karen the money not only to avoid taxes, but also to help her through school, so everything's fine. Five; if you give someone money, he or she is under no legal obligation to give it back. Never forget that! That ten thousand dollars is now Karen's.

"Now, let's move on to the second way the average Canadian can reduce his or her tax bill – become knowledgeable about all of the deductions and credits available to you! Before you start harping at me about not wanting to become accountants, let me add that to become knowledgeable in this area takes only a few hours of reading, not a few years of schooling. Just read your government-produced tax guide, and consider buying and reading one of the many available *Tax Tips* books. There are several of these easy-to-read books that list dozens, or even hundreds, of oft-forgotten potential deductions. James, for instance, didn't realize that he could claim tuition expenses for some of the correspondence courses he was taking, until he carefully read his tax guide. The tax savings amounted to hundreds of dollars."

"Doing the reading Roy is recommending may take five hours, but I'll guarantee you that you'll find at least one deduction that you haven't been taking advantage of. Your gains per hour of reading will be quite rewarding. And remember what a dollar saved is," James Murray reminded us.

"A final point about tax planning – "

"I thought the section on tax planning was supposed to be

as long as the section on investing," Tom chided Roy with a grin.

"You three didn't ask as many annoying questions during the section on tax planning. Besides, Tom, you're thinning up top," Roy shot back, also with a smile. "Now, I'd like to briefly discuss tax shelters. Technically defined, a tax shelter is any investment that enables investors to claim a deduction, loss or tax credit which may be applied to offset income from other sources. The tax deductions, credits or incentives won't usually cover the entire cost of the investment. So, if the investment proves to be a poor one, economic loss may result."

"Have you ever thought about writing a textbook, Roy?" Cathy teased.

"I realize that definition was somewhat technical, but it was also very accurate. I gave that definition to you so it would be clear to you that a tax shelter is nothing more than an investment. Yes, there are certainly tax implications, but all those tax considerations serve to do is to reduce your investment cost – your out-of-pocket cost. If the investment performs poorly, you could still be a loser despite the associated tax relief. Losing a dollar to save fifty cents is not an intelligent move.

"Why do tax shelters offer tax relief? Because, for the most part, if they didn't, nobody would buy them. The tax breaks serve as an incentive to buy – a needed incentive. That is to say that, by their very nature, tax shelters tend to be risky propositions. In addition to having a higher level of risk than most other investments, tax shelters are usually complex. Not only do you have to understand the tax implications, but you also have to understand the investment merits and you have to do battle with our old foe – timing."

"Are you saying not to ever buy a tax shelter, Roy?"

"No, I'm not saying that, but I am saying this: Before you ever buy a tax shelter, make sure you have seen a professional!"

"An investment expert or a psychiatrist?" I laughed.

"Both," Roy answered half-seriously. "And for heaven's sake, don't buy a tax shelter until the rest of your financial house is in order...no mortgage, a substantial RRSP, a growing ten percent fund, et cetera.

"I don't want to sound harsh here, but it's hard not to. For every success story in tax-shelter investing, there are nine horror stories. It's darn hard to figure out which tax shelters are going to be profitable! The prospectuses for tax shelters often read like the space-shuttle's owner's manual." Roy glanced at James Murray for support.

"Don't buy tax shelters!" James concurred with conviction. "I don't normally like to give blanket advice but, in this case, it's warranted. Sure, by following my advice, you'll occasionally miss out on a good investment – but you'll also miss out on dozens of bad ones. Believe me; I know!"

This particular advice was wasted on me. I have now, and had then, no intention of ever buying a tax shelter. I'd buy a bomb shelter first.

"So, what's on the agenda for our last month, Roy?" Cathy wondered. "The baby bonus and other miscellaneous topics?"

"Yes, there are three or four topics you still need a bit of information about. Then, of course, Clyde will present each of you with a hand-engraved, solid-gold plaque denoting your graduate status from the *Miller School of Financial Planning*. The plaque can either be wall-mounted or it can stand on a table – "

"Opportunistic pupils probably melt it down and sell it at the bank," interrupted the ever-enterprising Tom.

"I may have taught that lesson on thrift too well," Roy muttered, shaking his head.

10
GRADUATION

"Oh, you shouldn't have," Clyde protested modestly. "I really didn't do all that much."

"Something tells me that that beautifully wrapped package isn't for you, Clyde," speculated James Murray. "It's for me."

"Nice try, guys," I laughed. "This token of our appreciation is for Roy, in recognition of all that he has done for us. Admittedly, you two, and even Jimmy here, have also been big helps to us in our quest for financial independence. For all you've done for us, we'd like to present you with our heartfelt thanks. We were going to buy each of you a gift but as has been pointed out so often, 'A dollar saved is two dollars earned.' "

"Igor, vee've created a monster!" James Murray spoofed.

"You three really didn't have to buy me a gift," Roy blushed. "My reward is seeing you on the road to financial prosperity."

"That's exactly what I said, Roy, but Dave and Cathy wouldn't listen," Tom reported, straight-faced.

"Yeah, yeah...Dave, my boy, climb up into the chair and let's get started. There are four miscellaneous topics I want to touch on and then, of course, there's my world-renowned wrap-up speech."

"But James already delivered that rhetoric a couple of months ago, Roy. Can't we just skip your version?" Tom kidded.

"No," was Roy's concise response. "Now, it really doesn't matter which of the four topics we start with – "

"Back when we covered life insurance, you promised we would take a look at disability insurance this month," Cathy politely reminded Roy. "Let's talk about that first."

"Sure, Cathy," Roy indulged her. "Disability insurance is the most neglected of all forms of insurance, yet, for many people, it's the most critical insurance need. What are your chances of being disabled for a one-year period at some point in your life?"

"One in twenty?" Cathy guessed.

"I would say one in thirty," Tom speculated.

"One in four," Roy stated solemnly, taking the three of us aback.

Cathy broke our stunned silence. "That's amazing."

"It really is," Roy concurred. "A thirty-year-old has a one-in-four chance of becoming disabled for one year or more at some point in his or her life.

"At your age, your biggest asset, by far, is your earning power. You have to protect it. If a machine in your basement churned out forty thousand one-dollar bills a year, would you insure it against breakdown? Of course you would, especially if you knew there was a twenty-five percent chance that it would quit on you. Are you with me?"

We nodded our heads vigorously.

"When people die, they cease to be a financial asset to their dependents. That's why so many people need life insurance – to replace that asset – to replace that earning power. When people are disabled, they don't just cease to be an asset to their families – they become a liability. Excuse me for being blunt, but dead people don't need to be fed, clothed, or sheltered. Nor do they demand the constant medical care required by many disabled people. Make sure that you have proper disability insurance coverage!"

"I'm covered through work," I announced. "You probably are too, Tom."

"Be careful about that assumption, Dave," Roy cautioned. "Many employer group plans offer insufficient coverage. In addition, they are often non-portable. If you left your place of work to go out on your own or to go to an employer who did not provide adequate group disability coverage, you would have to hope that you were in good enough health to qualify for an individual disability policy."

"How can I tell whether or not my group plan is adequate?"

"It isn't easy. Disability insurance policies are complex. However, there are some basic questions that you should seek answers to.If you receive a *yes* to all of them, your policy would seem to be a good one. For example, is the loss of hearing, sight, speech or of the use of two limbs considered to be total disability under your group policy? Is disability defined in broad terms? Is the policy non-cancellable? Is there a waiver-of-premium clause? If so, does it extend beyond the benefit period? Is the only policy exclusion an accident of war? Does the policy provide benefits during rehabilitation? Are the benefits indexed?"

"Slow down, Roy! Where do we find out about all this?" Tom took the words right out of my mouth.

"Talk to your personnel department. They should know the answers to most of those questions and, if they don't, they'll know where to find them. Also, show your group policy to an insurance agent who can help you compare its pros and cons with those of an individual policy."

"What if our group policies are inadequate?" Tom pressed on.

"If your group policy is inadequate, Tom, or if you are not even a member of one, you will have to buy an individual policy. Most life insurance agents are well versed in the area of disability insurance. Moreover, there are agents who specialize in designing disability insurance programs. Either source should be able to advise you on the plan and options best-suited to your needs."

"How much coverage should we have?" I queried.

"Because benefits from disability policies are tax-free and because, for obvious reasons, insurance companies like to maintain a gap, an incentive if you will, between what you were making before being disabled and what they'll pay you while you are disabled, you're generally restricted to insuring between sixty and seventy percent of your gross income, less any benefits already in force."

"Is that a run-on sentence?" I asked, in my most formidable teacher-tone.

"What about car, fire and content insurance? Any advice in those areas?"

"Of course, Cathy. See your general insurance agent," Roy instructed her, with a friendly wink.

"Miscellaneous topic number two; saving for your children's education," Roy moved on. "Saving for your children's education is a relatively straightforward process – "

"It sure is, Roy," Tom interrupted. "Don't do anything and let the kids earn their way through school."

"How callous!"

"Not really, Cathy," I defended Tom. "There are all kinds of people, Mom and Dad among them, unfortunately, who believe that children should pay their own way through post-secondary school. I paid my own way and, although I wasn't too thrilled with our parents' stance at the time, I realize now that it was good for me. I learned the value of hard work and discipline. Today, I'm proud to say that I put myself through university."

"What a martyr," Cathy snorted. "The only reason Mom and Dad didn't help you out was that they thought you were going to flunk out."

If I hadn't suspected that to be the case, I would have offered a scathing comeback.

"Regardless of the parents' motives, as Dave said, there are all kinds of people who place on the child the responsibility of paying for a post-secondary education. In fact, I'm one of those people. However, I will admit that, for a variety of reasons, it isn't always possible for the student to shoulder the whole burden. A post-secondary education is expensive and even a hard-working, independent student can't always raise the needed funds. So, although I feel it's primarily the student's responsibility to put him or herself through school, I also feel that any parents worth their salt would help out, if necessary. Fortunately, putting yourself in the position of being able to help out is a very easy, and very inexpensive, part of financial planning.

"Dave, last month you were dying to discuss the baby bonus. Go ahead." Roy finally gave me the green light.

"Attribution rules don't apply to income earned by a child on family-allowance payments invested in his or her name." I impressed even myself with that succinct response. "Therefore, saving the baby-bonus cheques in the child's name is not only a good way to create an education fund, it's also very tax-effective. Because most children have no other taxable income, they'll often end up paying **no** tax on their baby-bonus investment returns."

"You've come a long way, kid," Roy congratulated me. "Now, forget the tax advantages of investing the baby bonus for one minute, and concentrate on two questions. One; do you think that you're going to miss thirty-two dollars a month, especially if you use the pay-yourself-first saving technique? Two; will a seemingly small investment of only thirty-odd dollars a month amount to anything much over the years?"

"No, we won't miss it!" I answered emphatically, "And yes, that so-called 'small' monthly investment will amount to something...something very substantial."

"How?" Roy prodded.

"Compound interest, that's how!" Tom leapt in. "The funds will grow reasonably well even if we don't invest the monthly cheques in ownership because they are likely growing tax-free."

"Compound interest, indeed!" Roy confirmed. "Your assertion that, even when invested in *loanership*, the baby-bonus money will grow nicely, is correct. However, I highly favour ownership. I mean, what better place for a PAC plan? Forced saving, dollar cost averaging, low PITA factor...it's perfect. What's more, we're looking at a nice, long term...say, fifteen years. By the way, why do I say fifteen years instead of eighteen?"

"I know!" Tom declared. "Murphy's law again! For the same reasons we don't want our RRSP dollars in equity investments just prior to buying a RRIF or an annuity, we don't want our education fund in equity funds just prior to our child going on to a post-secondary school. If the market were to take a dive, we wouldn't have the luxury of being patient. We'd be forced to cash out when the market was low. It's better to redeem the needed funds several years in advance, at a time when you see that the market is strong – sell high, you know."

"So, once our child is fourteen or fifteen, we should watch for an opportune time to redeem, do so, and then roll the funds over into guaranteed investment certificates," I summarized.

"That's right. And the nice thing is that the interest the GICs earn is taxable in the child's hands because the pool of capital has been created by saving the baby-bonus cheques."

"Roy, how much can I expect to save by investing Samantha's family-allowance cheques?"

"Making the fairly conservative assumption that the mutual fund will average thirteen percent a year over the fifteen years, and assuming an eight percent a year guaranteed return for the three subsequent years...hmm...somewhere in the area of ...twenty thousand dollars." James Murray's watch-calculator had come to our rescue yet again. "Naturally, after inflation, that twenty thousand will probably only be worth between five and ten thousand in today's dollars. Nevertheless, it will be a big help to Sam. In fact, combined with the savings from her own earnings and any government grants or loans she may qualify for, she should make it just fine. And, of course, being a child of yours, Dave, she's bound to earn a scholarship.

"Some of the people I've taught are taking it one step further," Roy continued. "Each month, they match the baby-bonus cheque with money of their own...thirty-two from the government, thirty-two from mom and dad."

"What about the attribution rules?"

"They don't cause much of a problem because, as I pointed out last month, the attribution rules don't apply to capital gains earned by a child. Admittedly, the mutual-fund holding does generate a small amount of dividend and interest income each year, and half of that amount must be claimed by the parent donating the matching thirty-two dollars. However, it's an insignificant amount."

"Why half?"

"Because the other half of the mutual-fund holding is from the baby-bonus money so, technically, it's the child's."

"Oh yeah, I forgot," I admitted, embarrassed. I had been on such a roll!

"A nice benefit of the *matching plan* is that, when the child is fifteen or so and the funds are cashed out, and the guaranteed investment certificates are bought, the attribution rules can again be circumvented. How? By purch – "

"By purchasing three-year compounding GICs," Tom interjected. "The GICs won't mature until the child is eighteen, so the interest earned, even on the half of the money donated by the parents, will be taxed in the child's hands. And since he or she will be at university, little, if any, tax will have to be paid."

I was finally ready to admit, not aloud mind you, that Tom had developed a sharp financial mind.

"Often grandparents want to help their grandchildren build an education fund. Matching the baby bonus is an excellent way," James Murray added.

"What do you think of Registered Education Savings Plans, Roy? Are they worthwhile?" My question elicited strange looks from Cathy and Tom, who must never have heard of RESPs.

"RESPs," Roy explained to my two baffled companions, "are registered plans to which you contribute after-tax dollars, meaning that you receive no tax deduction. However, with them, as with RRSPs, the government does allow investment earnings to accumulate tax-free while in the RESP. When your child enters a qualified post-secondary institution, an amount based on your total plan value is paid from the RESP to the child for each of the three or four years. That paid-out amount is then taxed in the child's hands."

"That's great!" I enthused. "Another way to income-split legitimately!"

"True," Roy said hesitantly, "but, in my opinion, sometimes not a very wise way. By using the three saving methods that we've just discussed – investing the baby bonus in the child's name, giving or lending your child money and investing it for growth, and buying compounding GICs with gifted money in the name of a child fifteen or older – you can not only save for a child's education, you can also save tax dollars. And none of these three methods exposes you to the risk that an RESP does."

"What risk? I thought RESPs were normally invested conservatively," I argued.

"What if your child doesn't pursue a post-secondary education? Then you'll receive only your RESP contributions back, and you will **not** get the earnings on them for the period your money has been in the plan. That kind of income-splitting, where it's your income that *splits,* is not recommended. Mind you, many financial companies are now offering very flexible RESPs that allow any number of beneficiaries per plan, and the beneficiaries can be changed at any time. Those same plans also often have very diverse investment alternatives. But, while there's no denying that RESPs are a much-improved product, I am still not totally sold on them."

"I decided against an RESP for my daughter because, at the time, I wasn't sure that she would go on to college or university. I analyzed the situation and reasoned that, for me at least, buying an RESP was too risky. I didn't want to lose the potential investment earnings."

I could see James Murray's point. Having a father who is a high school principal makes you acutely aware of the fact that less than fifty percent of the population goes on to post-secondary education. However, because RESPs have become so flexible, I'm still going to look into them.

"All right, onward we go. Miscellaneous topic number three;

emergency funds – "

"I was wondering when you would get around to that topic," Cathy jumped in. "Don't they always say that the average person should have a readily available emergency fund equivalent to three or four months' gross income?"

"Ah, the mysterious 'they' again," Roy sighed. "Many financial planners do recommend building and maintaining an emergency fund of that size, Cathy. Why? I don't know. To me, it makes little sense to have upward of ten thousand dollars sitting around earning fully taxable, low rates of interest. You would be much better off to use those funds to eliminate consumer debt or to fund your RRSP. Really, with the exception of a job loss or, for the business owner, an extended *down period*, what emergency could possibly call for ten thousand dollars?"

"What if the wind blows the roof off your house one night?"

"You're covered by insurance."

"What if your car breaks down and needs repairs?"

"Ten thousand dollars worth?"

"What if your furnace dies on the coldest night of the year?"

"Get it fixed," was Roy's uncomplicated advice. "It sure won't cost you ten grand. Look, I'm not against emergency funds, but I do feel that two to three thousand dollars is much more realistic than ten thousand. If you're afraid that an expensive emergency looms in your future, establish a ten-thousand-dollar line of credit at your bank. That way, if you really do end up needing the money, and I doubt that you will, it will be there for you. In the meantime, you're free to invest your funds in more productive ways.

"Having said that, let me repeat that it is important to keep a few thousand at your fingertips. Minor emergencies not only can happen, they do happen! Especially if you're a homeowner! Also, if you have a couple of thousand in the bank and you see some item on special that you really want, you can buy it. People with small bank balances are too often forced to pass up excellent bargains. And finally, having a couple of thousand in the bank is good for your peace of mind. People sleep less soundly at night knowing that they have only one hundred and sixty-eight dollars in their account."

"What do you mean, 'only'?" Tom chuckled.

"Roy, you mentioned that a business owner would be wise to have a substantial emergency fund. Does that include me?"

inquired Cathy.

"Obviously any business owner, or commissioned salesperson, whose income is unpredictable, varying widely over time, is smart to 'save for a rainy day.' It's surprising the number of stockbrokers, for example, who, during good times, raise their standard of living to match their temporarily-high income level, and don't set aside any funds to help carry them through the inevitable bad times. Cathy, whether or not your business is cyclical in nature is your call.

"People who have little job security are also smart to maintain a substantial emergency fund. Again, though, that decision rests with the individual involved."

"Another thing worth keeping in mind here, Roy," James Murray took over, "is human nature. All too often it subverts the purpose of an emergency fund. The temptation to convert the emergency fund to a travel or boat fund is just too strong for most of us. The old needs-versus-wants conflict again."

I could certainly see that happening!

"Miscellaneous topic number four; staying informed," Roy moved on efficiently. "Yes, your financial plans are very straightforward in terms of both implementation and maintenance. But it certainly can't hurt to keep abreast of the major goings-on in the world of finance. Certain events could occur that might dictate a change in your planning philosophy. For example, the individual managing your mutual fund could die. You might then want to re-evaluate your choice.

"As I said months ago, there are several excellent sources of financial information available in Canada, including the *Financial Times*, the *Financial Post* and the daily business section of the *Globe and Mail.* These publications aren't just informative; they're also entertaining. The world of finance is dynamic, colourful and fascinating!"

"Roy, can't you just do all the reading and keep us informed about anything pertaining to our financial futures?" Tom's idea sounded pretty good to me, but judging from the look of mock dismay on Roy's face, it didn't to him.

"All right, Clyde, drum roll, please. After seven long months, this is it. We've come to the end of the Miller course in financial planning. And, much to my delight, you have all passed with flying colours. However, before Clyde presents you with your diplomas, I'd like to make a closing remark...or two." Roy paused to step out from behind the barber chair.

"Over the last seven months I've taught you the basics of developing a productive financial plan. The strategies that I've outlined for you will serve well any Canadian between the ages of twenty and forty-five. They will do so regardless of occupation; regardless of income level; regardless of previous financial knowledge; even regardless of mathematical, investment and accounting skills.

"This comprehensive plan's strength lies in its simplicity. Anyone can understand and apply the principles that we've discussed. And, unlike most financial plans, ours goes beyond the mathematics of saving and investing to take into account human nature. Its success is not dependent on unrealistic expectations having to be met by the plannee, the way so many others are. I recognize that most people don't like to budget and that they don't enjoy constantly monitoring investments. I accept that most people enjoy blowing some money from time to time. I also understand that most people feel a great deal of stress when they are burdened with a high level of debt.

"The very simplicity of the plan troubles some people. 'How can anything so readily understood work so successfully?' It works because it is born of common sense. This plan allows us to move toward the attainment of all of our financial goals by taking advantage of unglamorous, but highly productive, concepts.

"Dave, when you first approached me, you said that you wanted to achieve the average Canadian's goals of a nice home, a prosperous retirement, an education for your children and, at some point, you wanted to enjoy the finer things in life. You wanted to accomplish this without having to be a financial genius, and without a substantial reduction in your current standard of living. Do you feel that you have learned how?"

"Mission accomplished," I acknowledged appreciatively.

"The bottom line is simply this," Roy concluded. "Fancy tax shelters, straddle-option strategies and future contracts on gold, all make for great conversation at cocktail parties. Forced saving, dollar cost averaging and compound interest simply make for great cocktail parties."

Roy's "bottom line," as he called it, was greeted with a standing ovation.

"Encore! Encore!" Tom shouted. "Teach us a family planning course now!"

"First, you'll have to find a wife, Tom. Now, please be seated,"

Roy protested. "Clyde, the certificates, please."

"You were serious about diplomas?" I asked, startled. "Wow, this is great! Hey, Tom, your first diploma!"

"Ha, ha!" Spending so much time at the barber shop had still not made Tom's comebacks razor-sharp.

Clyde proceeded to hand to each of us a beautifully framed, official-looking diploma from the *Miller School of Financial Planning*. He shook our hands and commended us for having taken the top three spots in our graduating class. Despite Clyde's kidding, the three of us were elated with our performance.

"As I'm sure you've noticed, we have a little something for you, too, Roy," I announced. Cathy presented Roy with a nicely wrapped package that obviously contained a framed picture.

Roy opened it deliberately, so as not to tear the gift-wrapping.

"Going to reuse that paper at Christmas?" James Murray joked. "The virtue of thrift, and all that stuff."

When the picture was finally visible to him, Roy's eyes became misty. My talented sister had painted the front view of Roy's impressive house, capturing it in the warm glow of a Lake Huron sunset.The engraved gold plate adorning the frame read simply, *The Rewards of Common Sense.*

"This is wonderful... I'm deeply touched... I just love it... My wife will want it hung in the main living room, for sure. You shouldn't have," an emotional Roy insisted.

"It was the least we could do for our financial mentor," I said sincerely. "We owe a great deal to you."

"In fact, we owe our good fortune," Tom smiled, "to **the wealthy barber!**"

The Wealthy Barber

Couldn't someone that you know benefit from reading *The Wealthy Barber*? It is the perfect gift for Canadians between the ages of 20 and 45 – understandable, enjoyable and profitable!

Please rush me _____ copies of *The Wealthy Barber* at $13.95 each, including shipping. I have enclosed a cheque made payable to Financial Awareness Corporation in the amount of $ _____ (Cdn.).

Full Name: _____

Address: _____

City: _____Province:_____

Postal Code:_____

Telephone #: _____

For an order of ten or more books we offer a discount. Please write to us for details, or call us at (519) 749-2164.

FINANCIAL AWARENESS CORPORATION
15 Duke Street East
Station B, P.O. Box 2781
Kitchener, Ontario
Canada N2H 6N3
Please allow four to six weeks for delivery.

The Wealthy Barber

Couldn't someone that you know benefit from reading *The Wealthy Barber*? It is the perfect gift for Canadians between the ages of 20 and 45 – understandable, enjoyable and profitable!

Please rush me _____ copies of *The Wealthy Barber* at $13.95 each, including shipping. I have enclosed a cheque made payable to Financial Awareness Corporation in the amount of $ _____ (Cdn.).

Full Name: _____

Address: _____

City: _____Province:_____

Postal Code:_____

Telephone #: _____

For an order of ten or more books we offer a discount. Please write to us for details, or call us at (519) 749-2164.

FINANCIAL AWARENESS CORPORATION
15 Duke Street East
Station B, P.O. Box 2781
Kitchener, Ontario
Canada N2H 6N3
Please allow four to six weeks for delivery.